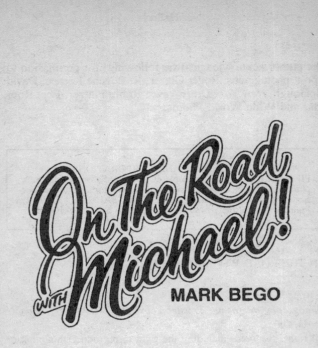

On The Road with Michael!

MARK BEGO

PINNACLE BOOKS **NEW YORK**

The author acknowledges [the following] for permission to reprint photographs: Roger Glazer, R. Eugene Keesee, David McGough, *New York Daily News*, Robin Platzer, Ebet Roberts, and Wide World Photos.

ON THE ROAD WITH MICHAEL!

An original Pinnacle Books edition, published for the first time anywhere.

First printing/December 1984

Printed in the United States of America

PINNACLE BOOKS, INC.
1430 Broadway
New York, New York 10018

To
MICHAEL JACKSON:
You are an inspiration to millions of children of all ages, all around the world. If more people shared your optimistic outlook on life, there wouldn't be so many problems on earth. You are THE star of the 1980s, the Thriller and Peter Pan all rolled into one. Your music and your moves are pure magic, so here's hoping you "Don't Stop 'Til You Get Enough"!

—M. J. Bego

ACKNOWLEDGMENTS

The author would like to thank the following people who in one way or another gave their time, energy, and/or support to this project:

Bob "Bandit" Anderson, Donna Anderson, Bart Andrews, Anne Bego, Catherine Bego, Gloria Bego, Mary Bego, Nancy Bego, Robert Bego, Frank Berk, Jane Berk, Fred Bernstein, Kevin Bezner, Susan Blond, Howard Bloom, Mike Bradley, Ginny Buckley, Barb Bullen, Robert Burns, Joe Canole, John Christe, Merry Clark, Richard Clark, Todd Coplevitz, Trippy Cunningham, Colin Curwood, Joe Dera, Jack Diamond, Lori Eastside, Howard Einbinder, April Eugene, Bick Ferguson, Susan Friedland, Neil Friedman, Sharon Ginzler, Roger Glazer, Ellen Golden, Steve Grad, Gary Graff, Victoria Green, Harry Haun, Andy Hernandez, Elliot Hubbard, LaToya Jackson, Ladonna Jones, Ed Katz, Don Kevern, Virginia Atter Keys, Janet Kleinman, Cash Landy, Mark Lasswell, June Lazerus, Elmer Luke, Steve Manning, Anne Marie McKenna, Brant Mewborn, Vesna Mezic, Gerri Miller, Ivy M. Miller, Skip Miller, Susan Mittelkauf, Jay Moore, John Morano, Marie Morealle, Kevin Mulroy, Jack Murphy, Cathy O'Bryan-Tear, Sondra Ordover, Beverly Paige, John Pemberton, Michael Peters, Bianca Pino, Robin Platzer, Ola Ray, Kenneth Reynolds, Richard Rinaldi, Sherry Robb, Rockwell, Steve Rothman, Kenneth Ross, Matt Roush, David Salidor, Bob Schartoff, Muriel Schwartz, Barbara Shelley, Linda Solomon, Carol Story, Anita Summer, Louis Tallerini, Alan Thicke, Josh Touster, Russell Turiak, John Warner, Dan Weaver, Miles White, Chris Wilson, Norman Winter, Bohdan Zachary, Pia Zadora . . . and special thanks to Peter Max

SOURCES

Material for this book was compiled from the author's first-hand observations and interviews, plus factual information from the following publications:

Billboard, *Black Beat*, The *Buffalo News*, *Cash Box*, *Daily Variety*, The *Dallas Morning News*, The *Dallas Times-Herald*, The *Denver Post*, The *Detroit Free Press*, The *Detroit News*, *Ebony*, *Fangoria*, The *Gazette* (Montreal), *The Hollywood Reporter*, The *Jacksonville Journal*, The *Jacksonville Times-Union*, *Jet*, The *Kansas City Star*, The *Kansas City Times*, The *Knoxville Journal*, The *Knoxville News-Sentinel*, *Life*, The *Los Angeles Times*, *Modern Screen*, The *New York Daily News*, The *New York Post*, The *New York Times*, The *Niagara Gazette*, The *Oakland Press*, *People*, The *Philadelphia Daily News*, The *Philadelphia Inquirer*, The *Rocky Mountain News*, The *Star*, *USA Today*, *U.S. News & World Report*, *Variety*, The *Washington Post*, The *Washington Times*

INTRODUCTION

For three consecutive months I attended every concert of Michael Jackson and the Jacksons' "Victory" tour of North America. I was at every one of the thirty concerts that Michael gave during the summer of 1984. It seemed like the only logical way to follow up my best-selling Jackson biography *Michael!* The book you are now reading is the result, and it picks up right where *Michael!* left off.

On the following pages, come along with me on Michael's triumphant Victory tour, to the Jacksons' Victory press conference at Tavern on the Green, to Michael's party at the American Museum of Natural History, to the 1984 Grammy Awards, to Michael's NAACP Award Presentation, and to every single Jacksons concert in twelve different cities. I was at every one of these events, and they are all detailed in this book.

If you were at any of the Victory concerts, you'll relive it in this book. If you didn't see Michael on tour in 1984, after you read this book you'll feel like you were there! It is now acknowledged that in twentieth century show business there have been four great phenomena: Frank Sinatra in the 1940s, Elvis Presley in the 1950s, the Beatles in the 1960s, and Michael Jackson in the 1980s. With his 35-million-selling international hit album *Thriller*, Michael has become the best-selling recording artist of all time. Michael's family reunion concert tour has been the grandest, most electrifying, most expensive, most profitable, most controversial, and most talked-about concert event in history.

Was it hype or was it a victory? I present both sides of the story—the positive aspects and the negative points. The triumphs, the confusion, the false starts, the excitement, and all of the controversy—I wrote about it all, the way that I saw it. From New York to Los Angeles to Kansas City to Dallas to Jacksonville to Newark to Knoxville to Detroit to Buffalo to Philadelphia to Denver to Montreal to Washington D.C., I have seen Michael in each of these cities this year. I have watched him win awards, and I have watched him win the hearts of millions of his fans.

As an entertainment journalist, traveling around the countryside covering Michael Jackson's Victory tour has provided me with the most exciting assignment of my life. These thirty concerts have been the equivalent of a solid month of the Thriller live and in person! In this book, join me on the road with Michael!

MARK BEGO
September 1984

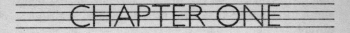

CHAPTER ONE

OPENING NIGHT: THE VICTORY TOUR

It is 7:30 P.M. on July 6, 1984, and I am sitting outdoors in Arrowhead Stadium in Kansas City, Missouri. It is a warm summer night, and in the seats surrounding me sit 44,999 other Michael Jackson fans, some of them wearing dark sunglasses, some wearing "Jacksons" T-shirts, and many wearing single sequined white gloves. People of every age, race, and nationality have flown in from all parts of the globe to be brought together in the middle of the United States to witness opening night of the most anticipated concert tour of the twentieth century. Tonight is the night that Michael reunites with his famous singing brothers for the first performance of the tour which appropriately bears the name "Victory."

Before me stands one of the tallest and most expensively constructed concert stages ever assembled. It was built to the exact specifications of Michael himself. It is the height of a five-story building, and to its right and left are gigantic murals painted on cloth, depicting two fully grown, multi-trunked trees whose tangled branches meet and drape their full green leaves onto a canopy over the stage. Beneath the

3

canopy of painted tree boughs are suspended 2,200 lights with various shades of colored gels, all pointed in readiness toward the floor of the stage. The weight of the sets and equipment is in excess of 750,000 pounds.

In the middle of the concrete floor of the stadium stands a tall scaffolding tower which houses video cameras, spotlights, and the lighting board. In front of it, on ground level and in select elevated areas, camera crews from every television network and major news service stand poised to capture on film each frame of this mega-event.

As the summer sun sets over the neighboring state of Kansas, Arrowhead Stadium begins to fill to capacity. For over two hours of recorded music, videos on a gigantic Diamond Vision screen, and a juggling act, I sit patiently sipping a Pepsi-Cola and watching the crowd. Finally, by 9:45 P.M. it is dark enough for the show to begin. After many false light cues, the houselights are lowered for the final time and the crowd screams, claps, and gasps, trying to imagine the spectacle they are about to witness. Suddenly my heart starts pounding, not knowing what to expect on the darkened stage before me.

To the sound of a sinister droning dirge, from out of the wings of stage left march five huge hunchbacked monsters known as "Kreetons." Over the loudspeakers, in a deep, low Darth Vader-like voice, a narrator begins, "Long, long ago, the Kreeton people walked half this earth, and they held the people captive for slaves in bondage, bringing evil and ruin to what was good. These are the Kreeton people." A glowing green iridescent boulder with a huge medieval sword sticking from it appears out of the darkness at the edge of center stage, and five knights of old march out and tug at the sword handle. The narrator continues, "Whoever would pull the sword from the stone would be king for years and years. It was prophesied that a mighty one would come and pull the sword from the stone and destroy the Kreeton people. This one would be called great, most holy and powerful. His kingdom shall be a kingdom that will never be brought to ruin; it will last from time indefinite till time indefinite. But who would pull the sword from the stone?" By this time all but one of the five knights have taken an unsuccessful turn at the sword, and the last one at that very moment withdraws the magical sword from the stone as King Arthur did with Excalibur. He wields it upward and points it toward the heavens. As he does so it glows an incandescent shade of green, and an incomparably impressive array of laser beams of red and green shoot into the stratosphere. The crowd screams with amazement at the incredible light show that dazzles our eyes. The knight swings the *Star Wars*-like laser sword menacingly at the Kreeton people, and all but one scurries for cover. "Destroy him!" commands a Kreeton voice. The knight and the last Kreeton do battle to a montage of music befitting a heroic deed in a Superman movie. Defeating the Kreeton, the knight in shining silver armor pulls off his helmet to reveal that he is Randy Jackson. As the Kreeton melts into the floor of the stage, Randy proclaims, "Arise all the world and behold the kingdom!" and runs off stage right.

As Randy disappears, laser lights flash and smoke begins to billow from the stage. The murals of the trees are pulled downward to reveal 120 custom-built speakers behind the skeleton of scaffolding to the right and left of the stage. As laser beams shoot out into the moonlit night sky, something begins to happen to the floor of the stage. A trapdoor rises up, bathing the stage and audience in hot white light. There, rising up from the opening in the stage, is a platform, and on it stand five figures bathed in white light. It is Michael Jackson and his brothers, freed by the knight's victory over the Kreeton monsters!

A seven-step staircase stands between the platform on which they are standing and the performing level of the stage. Taking each step in time with the adventure-film music that regally announces their arrival, the five Jacksons slowly descend to the stage. The audience is on its feet, screaming and applauding wildly, afraid to turn their heads from the stage for even a second. The hot backlights go down and the spotlights hit the Jacksons full on! There, in full view on center stage and dressed in a silver spangled jacket and black and white vertically striped pants, stands Michael Jackson. His outfit is completed by a sparkling white glove on his right hand and glittering white socks and black loafers on his feet. Across his chest he wears a regal red-sequined sash, as though he were European royalty as well as being the acknowledged crown prince of pop music. The crowd screams wildly at the sight of their idol.

All five brothers are sporting the dark sunglasses that they have recently made their trademark. They reach the floor of the stage, and in time with the music they all together remove their "shades" with a dramatic flourish. The crowd cheers loudly with unleashed excitement!

Band equipment glides onto the stage as if out of no-where, and the musicians dive into Michael's million-selling hit "Wanna Be Startin' Something." My heart kicks into full gear at the feeling of infectious ecstasy that is running through the crowd like lightning bolts. It is opening night at the biggest, most elaborate, and most talked about concert tour in history: the Jacksons' Victory. Here before me is the hottest, most successful musical superstar in the world—live and in person! Tonight is the single most exciting night possible in the life of any of Michael Jackson's millions and millions of fans—and I am there!

THE CONCERT OF CONCERTS

After all the talk, after all the problems and delays and speculation, the Jacksons are dancing in syncopation across the stage in Arrowhead Stadium. Michael is moving like the kinetic-energy dancing machine that the world has fallen in love with through his music and his videos, going into all of his mesmerizing dance steps while the sold-out crowd goes crazy! Grabbing the microphone and flashing an excited glance into the audience, Michael jumps into the song with a frenzy. While the thumping music plays, he swoops, he steps, and he poses from one side of the stage to the other, and executes a triple spin midsong that even the finest of whirling dervishes would be impressed with!

"Wanna Be Startin' Something" ends with all the Jacksons center stage. Randy Jackson, in a pose of sheer victory, holds the glowing sword toward the sky setting another breathtaking laser beam array flying off into the heavens. After striking this momentary pose, the group leaps right into their second song, "The Things I Do For You" from their 1978 album *Destiny*.

The show unfolds in a seamless stream of nonstop music, dancing, and special effects. Michael removes his flashy sequined outer jacket and bright red-beaded sash in midsong to reveal a collared white shirt decorated with sparkling rows of silver bugle beads covering its front, shoulders, and back yoke like a flashy version of a cowboy shirt. The number ends with all the brothers going into a simultaneous spin, to end up with their backs to the audience and their arms raised upward to form five identical V's for Victory. *"How do you feel? How do you feel?"* Michael shouts to the crowd.

At the height of a cheering ovation for "Things I Do For You," the Jacksons go directly into the title song of Michael's eight million-selling album, *Off The Wall*. The pace and excitement has yet to let up from the opening number! With Michael prominently in the foreground, "Off The Wall" gets a lively and moving interpretation. Finishing the song, the brothers take a quick breath and Michael asks the crowd, "How are you doing? Anybody here from Kansas City?" To which half the audience shouts an enthusiastic *"Yes!"* back at the gloved one.

As Randy Jackson plays the lone piano intro to Michael's number-one hit ballad "Ben," the crowd responds in favorable recognition. "Finally!" exclaims Michael, referring to the delayed opening night that the world had so long awaited. "The next one of my numbers," he continues, "is one of my favorite songs. It is an Academy Award nomination and a Golden Globe Award-winner. It's entitled . . . hold on . . . wait, wait, wait . . . hold on . . . wait!"

This is directed at Randy at the stage-left keyboards. Randy stops playing as Michael explains, "We've been doing this song for years and years. I'll tell you what. For a change...why don't you give me something new!" That exact second the band begins playing the top-ten smash ballad "Human Nature." While he sings, a live video camera projects close-ups of Michael on the huge televisionlike Diamond Vision screen above the stage. Laser beams of red and green hit a mirrored ball, sending spinning dots of confettilike laser light cascading into the crowd. The effect is brilliant.

As the song ends, the band plays the melodic synthesizer intro that leads directly into the group's hot dance hit from 1980, "Heartbreak Hotel." Demonstrating flashy choreographed moves center stage, Michael, Marlon, and Randy jump and strut about the stage with sweeping arm movements and enough pounding American Indian-style dance steps to conjure up rain! The fast-stepping trio is flanked by their older brothers, Tito and Jermaine, who are busily playing and swinging their guitars along with the song. Pyrotechnic effects explode in the middle of the number, and flames shoot up from the stage. Clouds of exotic light-catching smoke cover the stage floor, giving the entire elaborate visual presentation an ethereal aura that holds the audience in awe. The wild dance number ends with a soothing symphonic-sounding close, which shifts directly into the beautiful ballad "She's Out Of My Life."

While the stage glows with a royal-purple hue, Michael, in a sexy pink spotlight, begins to weave the sentimental song into a heartfelt rendition that has the audience hanging on his every note. Several girls in the audience emit shrieking squeals, as if they are about to swoon with elation.

"Can I come down there?" Michael asks the audience in the middle of "She's Out Of My Life," eliciting further audible waves of ecstasy at the thought that Michael might actually come down into the sea of fans! Moving far up to the edge of stage left, Michael continues singing while sitting with his legs dangling off the tall stage. Midsong he lies down on his back as though felled by the anguish of heartbreak over the girl in the song. The screams of teenage girls consistently punctuate Michael's ballad. Milking the song for all it's worth, he pauses at the end of the last verse, leaving the line "She's out of my . . ." unfinished for a full twenty-seven seconds as Michael wipes tears from his eyes, shielding his sight with the inside of his elbow. After many seconds of wild screams from the audience, he ends the song with an extended note-holding a cappella "liiiiiiiife." Al Jolson couldn't have sung the song any more emotionally!

As the beautiful ballad ends, wailing guitars and pounding drums change the mood. Wearing a sequined blue and purple striped cadet's jacket over tight pants, it is Jermaine Jackson at the guitar, playing the intro to his million-selling number-one smash "Let's Get Serious."

"Wait, wait, wait! Hold it! Jermaine, what are you doing?" Michael asks.

All the brothers begin to banter among themselves in mock disagreement.

"Fellas, I thought I was supposed to do my songs right here," argues Jermaine.

"You think you can come back and put your songs anywhere in the show? It just doesn't work that way," Marlon retorts.

The brothers debate. Tito wants to do the old Motown hits. Randy, Marlon, and Michael concur.

"I quit!" concludes an unamused Jermaine.

"I've heard that before!" Michael exclaims sarcastically, and then restores family harmony by mediating. "It's good to have you back," he tells Jermaine, "and we're glad you're here, and I tell you what. We'll let you do your songs—that's it!"

As Michael disappears from the stage after being the focal point of the show for over half an hour, Jermaine jumps into a rocking rendition of "Let's Get Serious." It is followed by his ballad from the Motown days "Do You Like Me," featuring a lushly soaring harmonica solo. Jermaine segues from the slow ballad directly into the opening bars of his 1984 radio smash "Tell Me I'm Not Dreaming (Too Good To Be True)," with Michael rushing out from the wings to do his solo part of the popular Jackson and Jackson duet.

The interaction between the brothers and the excitement of this song bring a cheering round of applause as it ends. The applause is then eclipsed by the screams and handclaps that ensue when Michael announces, "We're gonna give you the old stuff!"

They dive directly into their first Jackson Five hit, the million-selling number-one smash from 1969, "I Want You Back." It is performed in a Motown medley along with "The Love You Save," which is brought to life devastatingly complete, with all the original synchronized dance steps with which Michael and the Jackson Five introduced the songs almost fifteen years ago. Marlon, Randy, and Michael end the second song's final "Stop, the love you save may be your own!" with one hand extended palm out in a Supremes-like "stop" motion. The crowd goes bananas— we're all on our feet cheering and clapping along!

"You got it the old-fashioned way!" exclaims Michael as he completes the medley of Motown hits with the inspiring and soulful classic ballad "I'll Be There." There is more swooning and screaming as Michael revives the 1970 hit, with his four brothers all harmonizing. The crowd is thrilled as Jermaine, on stage with his brothers for the first time in over eight years, sings his solo lines. It is truly a night of musical history! Michael finishes off the song by singing a cappella and scatting into the announcement, "I think I want to rock!" Without a single pause, they jump directly into Michael's 1979 hit "Rock With You."

While a half-moon floats above in a clear blue star-dotted sky, on the stage below, which flashes with alternating blue and white lights, Michael Jackson continues to hold musical court for his enthralled fans. He ends the rocking up-tempo number with his arms stretched skyward in a symbolic V for Victory.

"Rock With You" is followed by the Jacksons' 1980 hit "Lovely One," which features Michael singing lead and unleashing some of his most mesmerizing choreography. The lively song has Tito and Jermaine wielding their guitars in sync while Marlon, Randy, and Michael launch into some of their most intricate interplays of outrageous dancing. The audience leaps from their seats screaming and cheering as Michael does his signature backward-gliding "moonwalk" at the edge of the stage.

The excitement is at its height at the end of "Lovely One," which is one of the hottest and most exciting numbers of the entire show. Suddenly Michael calls out to the audience, "Good night, everybody! Good night!"

All of us in the audience stare at each other in shocked disbelief. This could hardly be the end of the show we've all waited for for so long! Scattered applause and cheering punctuate the mystified opening-night crowd. Almost two full minutes of bewilderment come to an end as Michael begins scatting his way into his high-powered song "Working Day And Night." The whole entourage joins him back on stage amid a fantastic light show. Michael is now wearing a hot-looking and flashy red jumpsuit. Michael, Marlon, Tito, Jermaine, and Randy launch into a frenzy of syncopated dance steps that recharges the audience, which is still recovering from the oddly placed false exit that preceded the song.

Midway into the song, Michael calls out to guitarist Gregg Wright, "All right, Gregg, you've got it!" Wright launches into a fierce rock guitar solo with Jimi Hendrix-style musical and visual effects, playing the electronic instrument behind his back—and even with his teeth! The Jacksons' choreography follows the music into a rhythm of three-beat jumps, which concludes with Randy donning a sinister-looking silver mask and chasing Michael around the stage. The chase around the back of the huge drum set ends with Michael and Randy center stage.

Suddenly, eerie monster-movie music begins playing, and from the rafters of the stage two giant menacing eight-legged mechanical spiders descend toward Michael and the mysteriously masked Randy. With dozens of glowing light bulbs on their huge eight-foot-long legs, and a single twisting, blinking purple eye at the apex of their legs, the creepy octopods are obviously out to capture and consume a terrified Michael! He falls to the stage, paralyzed in horror! *"No!"* he repeatedly cries as one of the evil spider monsters closes its eight legs around him! Stunned by the grasp of the huge mechanical spider, Michael collapses on the floor of the stage.

Still wearing the spooky silver mask and a silver lamé cape, Randy removes the cape and covers his collapsed brother with it in magician style. A slablike platform rises out of the floor of the stage and lifts Michael's unconscious body upward. The outline of Michael's body continues to rise, hovering over the stage, covered by the silver lamé cape, as the spiders slowly disappear into the rafters from where they originally crept. Silence fells the crowd. No one knows what will come next!

Michael's body continues to rise, suspended over the stage. Randy then positions himself in front of cape-covered Michael, who is levitating above the floor of the stage. In a quick-handed and dramatic magician's move, Randy pulls away the silver cape and a flashpot explodes, casting a bright light on the stage to reveal that—Michael has vanished into thin air! The audience applauds the grand illusion. But what have Randy and the creepy space spiders done with our one-gloved hero?

Out of the darkness of stage left, another flaring pyrotechnic explosion blasts bright light over the stage, and all of a sudden a tall, elevated black box blasts open, and from within bursts Michael in a cloth version of the twenty-seven-zipper red jacket he made famous in the "Beat It" video. On the elevated platform Marlon stands next to him, posing with "attitude" while dressed in the dark glasses and white jacket of the gang leader character that Michael Peters portrayed in the same video. The band instantly hits the intro to "Beat It," and the audience screams with delight.

Moving about the stage in the same style of choreography that was featured in the video version of the song, Michael shimmies and sidesteps while the audience excitedly sings, shouts, and claps along. Gregg Wright launches into the spotlight guitar solo that was performed by Eddie Van Halen on the 35-million-selling album, *Thriller*. Michael dances alongside Wright while the guitarist plays the electronic instrument behind his back. Michael spins and jumps to the music of "Beat It" as flaming pyrotechnic special effects explode.

The audience goes into a rocking frenzy on hearing the opening bars of Michael's most famous international rock anthem. We are all on our feet and going wild!

After the pulsating drum-solo finale, Michael exclaims to a cheering standing ovation, *"How do you feel? How do you feel?"* The audience screams back a reply to him in excited adulation.

The stage lights fade to black, and when the spotlight next hits Michael, he is wearing the same loose-fitting black-sequined jacket and dark fedora he wore on the Emmy Award-winning television special "Motown 25!" Drummer Jonathan Moffett thumps out the beats of the intro to Michael's multimillion-selling hit "Billie Jean." Amid the song, while a half-moon peers out from a cloud high above Arrowhead Stadium, Michael dances to the edge of the stage and moonwalks backward *and* forward! The audience nearly has a heart attack at the sight of the break-dancing superstar.

At the end of "Billie Jean," a thunderous drumroll shakes the stage like an erupting earthquake. Giant wall-like banks of spotlights flash and move into new angles to point toward the audience, creating a much hotter lighting scheme as sizzling sparklers go off on stage. The crowd shrieks as Michael tosses his hat into the audience and the band swings into the biggest-selling hit single the Jacksons have ever recorded (2.5 million copies)—the funky dance tune "Shake Your Body (Down To The Ground)." The Jackson-crazed fans in the audience scream and shout with excited recognition! Taking their famous flashy choreography to new heights, the five Jackson brothers launch into the song with the enthusiasm that has made them famous around the world.

"Shake your body!" shouts Michael in a call-and-response fashion. "Shake your body!" Marlon, Randy, Tito, and Jermaine answer back. "Your mighty body!" Michael continues, with the crowd singing along. Sweeping and spinning across the stage, the baby-boom generation's Fred Astaire and his family dazzle the thrilled opening night crowd with stunning showmanship. Marlon calls out for the audience to put their arms above their heads in a V for Victory and to clap along. Michael scats and the audience shouts his "heee's" and "hooo's" back at him.

Posing together in a dancing huddle at center stage, the brothers move to the music in unison while a wave of shrieks and screams are emitted from the ecstatic sold-out crowd. "Good night, everybody! Good night!" shout the Jacksons as they dance offstage, each with his own physical flourishes to the music.

Suddenly, fireworks shoot overhead into the clear night sky just above the backstage side of Arrowhead Stadium. As the Jacksons disappear backstage, the band continues playing "Shake Your Body (Down To The Ground)" while the bright, colorful fireworks crackle overhead. The audience is on its feet in a cheering, screaming standing ovation. While the crowd roars with excitement, a black van speeds through an underground tunnel, whisking Michael and his brothers out of Arrowhead Stadium before the last of the fireworks explodes.

It is 11:30 P.M., and for the last hour and forty-five minutes Kansas City, Missouri, has witnessed the opening night of the most anticipated, grandest, most elaborate and exciting, most expensive and explosive popular music concert tour ever designed and executed. Michael Jackson and his four brothers have just written another record-breaking chapter in show business history before a cheering crowd— and I am part of it!

THE LONG ROAD TO KANSAS CITY

Many problems, setbacks, and complications preceded the Jacksons' triumphant opening night in Kansas City. The original plan was to open the tour around the end of May. However, after many false starts with various promoters, it was announced that the first concert would take place on June 22 in Lexington, Kentucky. But as the date drew near, the personnel involved in the planning of the Victory tour were making so many changes that it became clear there was no chance the elaborate show would be ready in time.

Finally, with football promoter Chuck Sullivan at the helm of the city-by-city planning and flamboyant boxing promoter Don King relegated to a figurehead role in the operation, things began to click. In late June it was announced that Michael and his brothers would utilize the June 27 to July 4 period for an extensive series of rehearsals in Birmingham, Alabama's Birmingham-Jefferson County Civic Center, and July 6 would become opening night in Kansas City, Missouri, followed by Dallas, Texas, and Jacksonville, Florida, on consecutive weekends. Further dates were to be announced prior to Kansas City.

The world was relieved to find out that the tour was indeed going to happen, and Michael, Randy, Marlon, Tito, and Jackie Jackson would soon reunite with their brother Jermaine in concert for the first time in eight years. The brothers finished work on the *Victory* album and set its official American release date at July 2. When the first single off the album, "State Of Shock"—featuring a duet between Michael Jackson and Mick Jagger—was released, it looked as if all the problems were over. But not quite.

On June 21 it was announced that the oldest Jackson brother, Jackie, would not be able to tour due to emergency knee surgery, and would have to be off his feet until at least September. It was decided, however, that the show would go on without him.

Then, to further complicate matters, a backlash of anti-Jacksons publicity grew out of the unprecedented ticket policy that would be implemented in the first three stops on the tour. An unusually high cost of $30 per ticket ($28 plus a $2 "handling fee") was set, with tickets to be sold by mail order only in lots of four seats per person. A certified money order for $120 had to be sent along with a special newspaper coupon to a post office box in New York City. Recipients of four tickets apiece were then drawn randomly by machine in a special lottery, and tickets would then arrive by mail. Those people who sent in $120 and didn't receive tickets were to have their money deposited into a bank account to accrue interest for the concert promoters, and their $120 refund check would arrive six to eight weeks later. To top things off, Chuck Sullivan began lining up stadiums that would rent out their facilities for a reduced flat fee, newspapers in the area of each concert were expected to run the coupons for free, and hotels that the Jackson entourage was to stay at were to reduce their normal rates for the Jacksons and their huge touring staff.

Unfortunately, the concert tour of the century was being described in terms of sheer greed, and suddenly the bad publicity was eroding all the good things that Michael had accomplished. Instantly, many of Michael's biggest fans were eliminated from being able to attend any of the concerts.

On June 20, 1984, it looked as if the Victory tour was going to meet its Waterloo as the stadium board members of the Chuck Sullivan-run Sullivan Stadium in Foxboro, Massachusetts (south of Boston), voted to ban Michael and the Jacksons from performing there for fear that the event would pose an uncontrollable security risk to the area.

In the first three cities on the tour, Dallas particularly, ticket sales were going very poorly. Had the *Titanic* of rock tours just found its iceberg? Searingly negative newspaper editorials made it clear that a backlash was well under way. Pure greed was the issue, and Middle America was unmistakably unamused.

It was painfully evident that the problems were stemming from the fact that there were too many chiefs and not enough Indians running this show, but it was going to be Michael Jackson, his popularity, and his fans who stood to lose the most. Something had to be done soon or the tour would be ruined from within. Not even the Kreeton people posed as much of a threat!

The last straw came from Dallas when a hurt eleven-year-old fan wrote an open letter to Michael Jackson. "How could all of you people be so selfish?" the crushed Ladonna Jones wrote to Michael, never imagining the impact her letter would have.

In Kansas City the day before the first concert, Michael Jackson himself stepped in and turned the tide by holding a press conference and announcing:

We're beginning our tour tomorrow and I wanted to talk to you about something of great concern to me.

We've worked a long time to make this show the best it can be. But we know a lot of kids are having trouble getting tickets. The other day I got a letter from a girl in Texas named Ladonna Jones. She'd been saving her money from odd jobs to buy a ticket, but with the current tour system she'd have to buy four tickets and she couldn't afford that. So I've asked our promoter to work out a new way of distributing tickets—a way that no longer requires a $120 money order.

There has also been a lot of talk about the promoter holding money for tickets that didn't sell. I've asked our promoter to end the mail-order ticket system as soon as possible so that no one will pay money unless they get a ticket.

Finally, and most importantly, there's something else I am going to announce today. I want you to know that when I first agreed to tour, I decided to donate all the money I make from our performances to charity.

"Magic" is one of Michael Jackson's favorite words. On July 5, 1984, by making the above statement, the mysterious young man with the sequined white glove had worked magic once again—and the Victory tour could at last live up to its name.

CHAPTER TWO

THE VICTORY TOUR PRESS CONFERENCE

I vividly recall the first time I heard about the Victory tour. It was in October 1983, only weeks after I had completed writing the book *Michael!* In the October 31, 1983, issue of the *New York Post*, columnist Cindy Adams reported, "Michael Jackson, the 25-year-old hottest name in music whose last album sold 14 million copies, is getting back together with his old family, The Jackson Five. Boxing promoter Don King has just promoted this knockout of a deal to launch his own entrance into the music business. . . . In six months King did what Kismet couldn't do in five years. He signed all the Jacksons to go on tour together. . . . This, possibly the biggest concert tour ever, will be in '84. It'll be 40 dates. It'll kick off domestically, then go international. It will be sponsored by one of the largest corporations in the United States."

And so began a month of rumors, speculation, and hype. In the beginning weeks of November, it was announced that a massive invitation-only press conference would be held at the lavish restaurant in Central Park, Tavern on the Green. Every press member that I know was vying for one of the engraved invitations for what was being termed "Michael Jackson's press conference." However, I distinctly remember the whole event turning into "Don King's press conference—featuring Michael Jackson." The invitation itself read:

Don King
and
Katherine and Joseph Jackson
cordially invite you to join the entire
Jackson Family
for a Special Press Announcement
of
"The Union and Reunion"
Wednesday, November 30, 1983
12:00 noon
Tavern On The Green

Riding in a taxicab from my office at *Modern Screen* magazine to the event that cold November morning, I was surprised to see the police barricades that blocked every entrance to Central Park. Policemen in riot helmets, police vans, and policemen on horseback were stationed and ready for any trouble they might encounter from hordes of crazed Michael Jackson fans. A whole section of the park was sealed off from the public.

There was only one way into Tavern on the Green, and when I arrived there at 11:30 there was already a restless mob at the door—and these were just the members of the press! Finally, after a brief wait invited guests who had an invitation and whose names also appeared on a special list were allowed inside.

Stepping over television and radio cables, I was directed to the glassed-in Crystal Room of Tavern on the Green. In the center of the room was a roped-off area with tables and chairs set up for special guests and Jackson family members. At the innermost end of the room a speaker's podium with microphones had been set up, and alongside it was a long table with six chairs and six microphones, obviously for the six Jackson brothers to speak from.

Over the next hour the room swelled with every entertainment reporter and photographer within a thirty-mile radius. While inside everyone was jockeying for a good position from which to view the event, outside the sun kept breaking through the clouds and casting beams of light through the many cut-crystal chandeliers in the room.

It wasn't long before members of Don King's family took their places at tables in the roped-off VIP area. They were soon joined by LaToya Jackson, Katherine and Joseph Jackson, little sister Janet Jackson, and all of Michael's sisters-in-law. Also present were singing stars Patti LaBelle and Roberta Flack, noted actors Ruby Dee and Ossie Davis, and celebrated artists Andy Warhol and Peter Max.

The anticipation of Michael Jackson's entrance was so thick it could have been cut with a knife. However, there was quite a wait for his brief appearance. At long last the event got under way as Don King appeared at the podium with his trademark hairdo greying and standing straight up on end as if he had just received high-voltage electroshock therapy.

Began King, "Welcome to the Tavern on the Green. We are delighted to have you. We have, as you know, and I guess you're all aware, a very exciting announcement. But we're going to make this program a little informative for you so you will understand what's about to transpire. It's euphoric, it's exciting, it's heavy, it's the Jacksons. . . ."

First he talked about promoting prizefights, then he went on to expound on the importance and definition of the family in society. He went on to describe all the Jackson family members, going on and on about his business deal with Michael's parents, Katherine and Joseph Jackson. Lengthy introductions also went to distinguished members of the audience, including many sports figures and members of his own family. Next he read off the entire twenty-year history of the Jackson Five, ending by paraphrasing a speech that Malvolio gave in Shakespeare's *Twelfth Night* which read, "Be not afraid of greatness. Some men are born great. Some achieve greatness. And others have greatness thrust upon them." King drew a correlation between the speech and the Jacksons, and talked on and on and on. Then he showed a videotape about himself! The press was having a fit of restlessness. Twenty minutes of solid speeches, and still no Jacksons!

Finally a backdrop parted and a stage set was wheeled in that resembled the front porch of a country farmhouse. Michael, Marlon, Tito, Jermaine, Jackie, and Randy Jackson stepped off the set and took their places at the long table with the six microphones. At that moment, Don King introduced Roger Enrico, president and chief executive officer of Pepsi-Cola U.S.A.

Enrico went on to announce that the Jacksons' tour would be sponsored by Pepsi and the Jacksons would be doing television commercials for the company. Finally, Don King introduced the Jackson brothers and invited questions from the press. Throughout the proceedings, the six Jacksons sat quietly behind their identical dark sunglasses.

The quickly answered questions established that Pepsi had initially invested $5 million in the Jacksons and that the tour would begin in the United States in the summer of 1984 and encompass a possible world tour. Michael, who had not uttered a single word throughout the entire press conference, finally spoke up and began in his softest voice, "I can't really say much today, but I would like to introduce my family . . ." Throughout, Don King would butt in and repeat Michael's introductions. King added, "Michael's voice is a little strained from making all those hit records, and he won't be able to answer any more questions today."

All told, the press conference was thirty minutes of Don King, and thirty seconds of Michael Jackson! But one thing was established that afternoon, and that was that the biggest and most widely anticipated concert tour in history was about to be embarked upon.

At the press conference that day, I personally suspected that there might have been a bit of friction between the King company and the Jackson family. It appeared that Michael and his brothers were present only to embellish Don King's enterprise. Later developments proved my suspicions to be correct.

After that November press conference, no official announcements were made with regard to the tour. However, throughout December Michael managed to stay in the forefront of the news, and the publicity did nothing but enhance the most successful year of his twenty-year career.

THE "THRILLER" VIDEO

As though what Michael Jackson had accomplished with his video versions of "Billie Jean," "Beat It," and "Say, Say, Say" was not keeping his fans excited enough, December 1983 saw the release of the most fantastically conceived and brilliantly executed music video yet: "Michael Jackson's 'Thriller!'"

At the cost of $800,000 the fourteen-minute Jackson video is a mini-monster movie with great dancing, incredible makeup and special effects, and excellent cinematography. Michael personally chose John Landis to direct "Thriller." Landis is famous for his imaginative *American Werewolf in London* and his controversial segment of *Twilight Zone— The Movie*. The ensemble choreography was done by Michael Peters, who worked with Jackson on the video "Beat It," and the outrageous monster makeup was done by Rick Baker, who won an Academy Award for his work in *American Werewolf in London*.

The video opens with the written disclaimer "Due to my strong personal convictions, I wish to stress that this film in no way endorses a belief in the occult.—Michael Jackson." Due to Michael's strong religious conviction as a Jehovah's Witness, he was very concerned that he not offend anyone by turning into a catlike werewolf and ghoul in the film.

It debuted on MTV on December 2, 1983, and that same

month saw the release of the hour-long documentary video cassette (and video disk) "The Making of 'Michael Jackson's "Thriller,"'" distributed by Vestron Video. The video presentation went on to sell in excess of 500,000 copies in its first month of release. "The Making of 'Michael Jackson's "Thriller"'" also includes excerpts of Michael's Emmy-nominated performance of "Billie Jean" from the TV special "Motown 25," excerpts from "Beat It," the Jacksons' video "Can You Feel It," and interviews with John Landis, Michael Peters, Ola Ray, Rick Baker, and many of Michael's fans. There is also footage of eleven-year-old Michael in the early 1970s with the Jackson Five from TV's *The Ed Sullivan Show*. One of the most fascinating segments demonstrates how the incredible makeup effects were created and how many of the special effects were achieved during the filming.

According to Rick Baker, his involvement in "Thriller" began with a phone call. "John Landis was in London at the time," he explained recently. "He called me and said, 'Hey, guess what—I got a call from Michael Jackson, and he wants to do a video for his song "Thriller." He wants me to direct it, and he wants to be turned into a monster in it, so I want you to do it.' Michael had seen *American Werewolf* and really liked it, so he wanted to make something scary, and wanted to change into a monster. Landis sent me a copy of 'Thriller' and I listened to it and listened to it, and put together some ideas, things I'd like to try. At the time, I thought it was going to be something along the lines of a standard rock video."

Continued Rick, "John came out to L.A., we had a meeting with Michael, discussed our ideas, and then John went off and wrote the script. We had come with some ideas that I found pretty exciting, particularly the dancing zombies. For a long time I've wanted to do a straight horror film with some zombies in it that would, at some point in the middle of the film, break into a song and dance. . . . I'd wanted to talk Michael out of the transformation, just because so many of them had been done, even on TV with *Manimal*. Michael, though, was really set on turning into a werewolf. At least I was able to talk him out of going for a normal werewolf. I suggested a more catlike creature, which I thought was more appropriate for Michael, and at least it was something slightly different that would allow me a little more fun with the design. Michael liked that idea."

"Early on, I'd suggested a couple of winged demons," recalled Baker, "and Michael said definitely no demons. So I had reason to doubt that he'd want to turn into a really monstrous monster, and the original concept I had for this was a sort of demonic cat monster. After Michael said no demons, my design sketches were a pretty sort of black panther monster."

Said Ola Ray of her role in "Thriller," "It was hard work, but it was also a lot of fun. I learned a lot from both Michael and John Landis. It was great." The pretty twenty-three-year-old actress recalls of her audition for the part, "I figured, well, I'm going to audition for a Michael Jackson video, big deal. If you're an actress, it's easy to become callous about auditions, because you don't get every role you go up for. But when I met with John Landis and found out that whoever got the part would play Michael's girlfriend and that the video would cost so much, I got excited. It's always hard to tell, but when I met with Landis, I felt I'd already gotten the part!"

Oddly enough, Ola's biggest recognition had been as June 1980's *Playboy* magazine centerfold Playmate. Apparently Landis convinced Michael that Ola was a very sweet, down-to-earth girl, and her nude centerfold didn't upset him and his devout religious beliefs. Says Ola of Michael, "He's a perfectionist for sure, but he was always very friendly with the dancers and the crew. He's a practical joker. He kept saying, 'I can't wait until I do the werewolf scenes so I can chase you.' I'd say he is shy, but only when he's around people he doesn't know. Actually, Michael seems almost outgoing, at least while he's working. I could tell just by the way he playfully flirted with me that he likes women. I met Jane Fonda at the studio while getting my makeup done and she asked me to take him a note and give him a kiss and hug. When I told Michael about the kiss, he said, 'Well...!?' I think if he finds the right girl, he'll marry her. But in the meantime, I just don't think he deals with sex. He seems to be on a different level. I mean, sex isn't everything."

On May 30, 1984, I interviewed choreographer Michael Peters for *Modern Screen* magazine with regard to his involvement as co-choreographer of "Thriller." Our conversation went as follows:

BEGO: How were you brought into the "Thriller" video?

PETERS: Initially when Michael Jackson talked to John Landis, he wanted to choreograph it himself. John said, "Well, I think it's a big undertaking. You know, maybe it would be wise to have somebody on the other side of the camera." I actually did choreograph it. It was just that he wanted to feel that he had creative control. Because basically he did his solo stuff. If you split it up it would be 85 percent [Peters], 15 percent [Jackson] as to who did what. It ultimately became of little importance, because it was on the screen, and there it was! He obviously needed that at the moment, and, great! We worked a day together, and then the second day when we were supposed to continue working when the dancers came in, he had to spend that day with his makeup, so he couldn't create, so I just went ahead and did it.

BEGO: When you were working on "Thriller," did you work on steps that were easy to synchronize but looked menacing for the monsters and decayed people?

PETERS: Actually, I just sort of thought of the sickest things I could do! *(Laughing.)* No, really! All the people I called were people that I knew were really mad! And I said, "This is not a glamour gig. If you want to come and play and just be sick—this is it!" I gave them all the choice of characters.... I brought in prototypes of the masks and all that stuff. "This is what it's gonna be like, and this is what you're gonna be in. And if you're not into it, it's fine, just let me know now, and I'll call somebody else." And everybody went, "Give me that mask!" The more crazy we got, the more things we kept!

BEGO: So you did the casting of the dancers?

PETERS: Yes, I had asked Michael Jackson if he had any preferences to how many men and how many women. Originally, I think he wanted all men. I had just done Pat Benatar ["Love Is A Battlefield" video], so I showed him Pat Benatar, and I said, "Yeah, we should have some ladies in it." He was working on "Say, Say, Say" [the video], so I just went ahead and hired all the dancers, and they were all there when he got there.

BEGO: Both videos were being filmed around the same time, weren't they?

PETERS: Yes, October 1983. He finished one on one day and started "Thriller" on the next.

BEGO: Did you work on any of the nondancing movement in the "Thriller" video?

PETERS: No, they had actually rearranged the whole shooting schedule, because I was getting ready to direct *Fame* [a segment of the TV show], and I could only work on two days, which was the allotted time for the dance sequence, so I didn't work on any other part but that segment. I was actually supposed to be there when he and Ola walked down the street, leading into the monsters, but I just didn't have the time, so he did it.

BEGO: In the terms of a dancer, would you say that Michael Jackson is the 1980s version of Fred Astaire?

PETERS: I think he's got the gift. You either have it or

you don't. He's always had it. I think like anything or anybody, the more exposure he has to
different elements of that arena, he will grow.
If he should so desire to do a Fred Astaire type
of number and study that form of movement,
that will just add to what he does, because he
has the wonderful ability to imitate what he sees.
He's a chameleon of sorts, and that's one of his
powers that, although he has no technical
knowledge of what it takes to do, plus the soul,
he can imitate—whether that's by rhythm or in
the mirror, emulating style, or the line of the
movement. So, I think he's the type of person
that whatever he chose to do, he would go ahead
and do that.

BEGO: You're the first choreographer to work with him
on that basis since the Motown days of the Jackson Five. Are a lot of his dance steps derived
from those that his days at Motown taught him?

PETERS: Yes, also the stuff that he did when he was little.
That audition tape that they show of him in the
basement was all the stuff that James Brown
used to do [referring to a flashback segment of
"The Making of 'Michael Jackson's "Thriller"'"]
I think that it's like any of the people that I've
worked with. If you challenge them to grow,
they'll do it. And it's the same with Michael
Jackson. He could have been left to do what he
does and been very very successful and always
been acknowledged for that, but I think the fact
that he took the chance to try something a little
bit different, a little bit new, and grow and expand, has taken him to another level. He's an
innovator. If he chose to do ballet, he could do
it—I really believe it!

Michael Jackson closed 1983 on top of the world. The
last week of the year, his duet single with Paul McCartney,

"Say, Say, Say," was number one on the singles charts (making it his seventh top-ten single of the year), and *Thriller*, having spent all fifty-two weeks of the year in the top ten, was the number-one album. In fact, in 1983 *Thriller* became the first album in the history of recorded music to start a year number one, and end number one the same year.

By December 31, 1983, at over 20 million copies sold, *Thriller* had become the second largest selling album ever, right after the soundtrack to the movie *Saturday Night Fever*, and it was still selling!

As 1983 ended and 1984 began, Michael Jackson was the undisputed top entertainment figure in the entire world. On New Year's Eve, millions of people around the globe welcomed in 1984 dancing the night away to the sounds of Michael's "Billie Jean," "Wanna Be Startin' Something," "Beat It," and "Thriller." 1983 was just the beginning of Michael Jackson mania, as his popularity continued to soar at an astronomical rate.

CHAPTER THREE

THE AMERICAN MUSIC AWARDS

The shaping of 1984 into the year of Michael Jackson began merely hours into the calendar. On January 3 in Hollywood, it was announced that Michael Jackson led the distinguished list of nominees for the Eleventh Annual American Music Awards. With a total of ten nominations spanning every category of eligibility, it was clear from the start that this year's awards would be dominated by the Thriller himself.

Michael was nominated for the title of the year's top Pop/Rock Male Vocalist, Pop/Rock Single ("Billie Jean"), Pop/Rock Album (*Thriller*), Pop/Rock Video ("Beat It" and "Billie Jean"), Soul Male Vocalist, Soul Single ("Billie Jean"), Soul Album (*Thriller*), and Soul Video ("Beat It" and "Billie Jean"). To top it all off, it was announced that he was also set to receive the year's Award of Merit for "outstanding contributions over a long period of time to the musical entertainment of the American public." Let's face it. Can you think of a more deserving recipient than Michael Jackson?

The American Music Awards began as a mere premise for Dick Clark Television Productions to have a glitzy annual TV special without having to deal with any existing unions or music associations for validity. Nominations are culled from the nation's music trade publications and are submitted to 20,000 consumers selected in a national sampling. The data is then compiled by the Herbert Altman Communications Research firm, and they determine the winners. Although the American Music Awards aren't affiliated with any official music industry entity, they serve as an apt thermometer of the past year's musical fads, trends, and tastes. Whatever the purpose, the televised, star-studded event is usually the most entertaining and well produced of all the yearly awards shows, and in 1984 it aptly heralded Michael Jackson as the undisputed entertainer of the decade!

Telecast live from the Shrine Auditorium in Los Angeles on Monday, January 16, 1984, the eleventh edition was an exciting evening for Michael's millions of adoring admirers across America. That night the American Music Awards were dubbed "The Michael Jackson Awards!"

Presenting the first award were Melissa Manchester and Kenny Loggins. When the award for Favorite Pop Single was presented, Melissa announced, "And the winner is . . . [opening envelope] 'Billie Jean,' Michael Jackson!" The audience went wild with screaming and applause. For those of us viewing the event on TV, we got our first full shot of Michael as he stood and walked up to the stage. He was wearing a red bugle-beaded jacket with beaded gold epaulets, gold braid around the collar, five cords of gold braid across the front of his jacket, and a gold bugle-bead-covered sash with silver stripes extending from his right shoulder down to his left hip. He was wearing black peg-legged tuxedo pants that stopped at the ankle to expose silver bugle-beaded spats over black shoes. On his right hand was a black-beaded glove, and on his head were black-lensed aviator sunglasses. Until this point in the telecast we had only viewed Michael in the front row of the audience seated next to his date for the evening, Brooke Shields.

Bounding up the seven steps to the stage amid the screams of the audience, Michael turned and waved to his fans.

Approaching the podium, Michael slapped the palms of Kenny Loggins' hands in a congratulatory gesture, took his award, and kissed Melissa Manchester on the cheek. Melissa turned her cheek to the audience, pointed to the freshly kissed spot, and gave a "Look what I just got!" expression as the fans shrieked.

Michael waved his black-gloved hand again and accepted his award by modestly saying, "I'm very thankful, and I'm very honored for this award, and I don't want to make a long speech. I'm just...thank you very much." With that he exited the stage.

Our next glimpse of Michael came after Lionel Richie announced, "To present the award for Favorite Soul Album, here are two exciting new stars: Favorite Soul Female nominee Angela Bofill, and a young man who 'cuts like a knife,' Bryan Adams."

After Bryan read off the nominees, Angela opened the envelope and announced, "And the winner is: *Thriller*, Michael Jackson!"

Again striding up those seven steps to the podium, Michael took his second 1984 American Music Award by saying, "Thank you very much. I'm deeply moved again to win this award. I'd like to thank Quincy Jones, for he's a wonderful producer...and my mother and father who are in the audience whom I love very much, who brought me into the world. And I also thank the American public. Thank you." With that he waved his black-gloved right hand, turned, and exited.

The next award was for Favorite Pop Album, and the winner was naturally Michael Jackson's record-setting *Thriller*. Amid more screams of ecstasy from the audience, Michael gratefully took his trophy and expressed his gratitude by saying, "Again I...I'd like to thank everybody. I'm deeply moved by accepting this award, and it was so much fun doing the album *Thriller*, and I'd like to thank again Quincy Jones, and Bruce Sweiden who is the greatest engineer in the world, and also Rod Temperton and James Ingram for writing 'P.Y.T.' with Quincy Jones...thank you. And again my mother and father who taught me so much, and..." at which point a girl in the audience yelled out, "I love you Michael!" Michael blushed, beamed a wide smile, scratched his head, and then ducked down behind the podium for a second to shyly acknowledge the screams and applause that punctuated his entire speech. He continued, "And again I'd like to thank the disk jockeys who play the records, because if it wasn't for them we wouldn't be heard. And I also would like to thank the public. Thank you very much." About this time, all across America people were wondering, "What is with the dark glasses? Why doesn't he take them off? This is his night, why is he hiding behind the shades?" Michael held up his award, an engraved crystal obelisk, in a triumphant gesture, and the camera cut to Brooke Shields clapping in the audience.

After Rick James and his girl group, Mary Jane Girls, presented Alabama with the award for Favorite Country Album, Lionel introduced Kenny Rogers as 1983's winner of the American Music Awards' Award of Merit. Taking center stage, Kenny launched into his tribute to this year's winner, and for the next twenty minutes Michael Jackson was lauded for a lifetime of achievements.

Kenny began by stating, "This year's recipient of the Award of Merit, at twenty-five years old, is the youngest person to ever receive this award. And for twenty of those twenty-five years, he has been an outstanding performer. And today, without a doubt, he is the most talked about performer in the world. In fact you might say, 'He's a thriller!'" With that, footage from the "Thriller" video was brought up on the monitors.

Continued Kenny while the musical track of "Thriller" played in the background, "Here's the thrilling facts about Michael Jackson's *Thriller*. It's the first album to ever be number one in the American pop, soul, disco, and European charts all at the same time. It's the first album to start the year number one, and end the year number one. It's the first album ever to contain six hit singles—a world's record. And it has now sold almost twenty-five million copies worldwide and may soon be the biggest album in history. Michael is the biggest success story since Elvis and the Beatles. His success didn't start yesterday. Just look at these fifteen years of American Music Awards, Grammys, video awards, NAACP Entertainer of the Decade award, and so many awards."

Over a further montage of video footage, Rogers narrated, "From 1969 until 1976, the Jackson Five and Michael alone recorded a total of eleven albums and had four number one hit singles in a row. All in all, during their years at Motown, Michael and the Jackson Five sold over one hundred ten million records. In 1976 they became the Jacksons and moved to Epic Records with even greater success."

What followed were taped and live tributes to Michael by some of his closest colleagues and friends: Quincy Jones, Liza Minnelli, Paul McCartney, Yul Brynner, and Emmanuel Lewis. Barry Manilow then played and sang a musical tribute to Michael.

After an orchestral crescendo to "I'll Be There," Barry said, "You know, Michael has many friends in show business, but there's one who occupies a very special place . . ." at which point footage of Diana Ross and Michael from her 1980 television special was shown. "Ladies and gentlemen . . . Miss Diana Ross!"

Dressed in a full-length gold lamé dress, Diana sashayed onto center stage amid wild applause. Diana said, "I know you know that Michael and I are like family. We've shared many magic moments together—the early days, and television specials, recording and doing the movie *The Wiz*. Well, you know Michael; he's an exceptional human being, talented beyond his years, a dream in motion. I wish Berry Gordy was here tonight to share in this presentation. I'm sure he remembers Michael's Emmy-nomination performance on 'Motown 25,' dancing and singing to 'Billie Jean.' Let's see a little of that," at which point the much-heralded clip from the 1983 television special filled the screen.

As Michael stood to ascend the seven stairs to the stage to join Diana, he elicited screams and shrieks of ecstasy from the audience, which leaped to its feet in a cheering, standing ovation for the man who had virtually dominated the show with his presence and his unprecedented number of victories. Reaching downstage center while the constant beat of the song "Billie Jean" played, Michael went into a swooping, spinning dance step from his video of the same name.

By this time, Quincy, Kenny, and Barry had emerged from the wings of the stage to stand stage right of Barry Manilow's clear lucite grand piano. Walking upstage to join them, Michael took the wireless microphone from Quincy and gave the three men big hugs of appreciation. And then he finally gave a huge bear hug for Diana, who continued, "Michael, we're honored to present to you American Music Awards' Merit of Honor." Then laughingly correcting herself, she said, "Actually the Music Award of Honor, and well, I'm very proud of you—congratulations!"

"Well, thank you," said Michael shyly as Lionel Richie handed him the crystal obelisk-shaped award. Without removing his dark glasses, Michael continued, "Thank you very much. I'm so deeply touched and deeply honored to receive this wonderful—gosh—this wonderful award. I thank the American public, I thank Berry Gordy of Motown, who has been such an important part of my career and life. I thank again my mother and father who brought me into the world: Joseph Jackson and Katherine Jackson." At which point the pair was picked out of the audience by the cameras. "I thank all of my brothers: Tito, Jackie, Jermaine, Marlon, and Randy, who I started with, and still am with. I thank Suzanne DePasse, who has been such an important influence in my life and who has taught me so much [referring to the Motown Productions executive who produced the "Motown 25" special and many other creative projects for that company and its acts]. Thank you, Suzanne."

Placing his black-sequined gloved right hand around the shoulder of Quincy Jones, Michael continued, "Quincy Jones is a wonderful person. Not only is he an incredible producer, he is a wonderful man. He is such a family person, and I love him, and we have made history together, and I'm thankful."

Embracing Diana, Michael said, "I thank one of my favorite people in the whole entire world, Miss Diana Ross. She's been such a special friend to me and has taught me so many incredible important things, and I'm just so honored that she came here." To which Diana laughingly interjected, "And taught you how to dance, right?" Michael went on to state, "I just hope I didn't leave anybody out. I just — boy — the American public, and I thank all the disk jockeys, and everybody. I love you so much, and thank you." Taking a swooping bow of appreciation to the standing ovation, Michael shot his black-sequined gloved hand skyward in a triumphal salute. While the cheering continued, Michael took the trophy from Lionel Richie and struck a pose with it, to more screams from the crowd.

After Michael's "Beat It" proceeded to win Favorite Soul Video and Favorite Pop Video, Lionel Richie joked to the crowd, "You know, what we might have to do here is get the ushers to kind of clean out the seats around Michael so he can put his awards down. Do you think that's possible?"

Michael's seventh award of the evening was in the category of Favorite Soul Male. As he ascended the stage this time, Michael was followed up the steps by his little friend, Emmanuel Lewis, who was dressed in a tiny tuxedo with tails. At the top of the steps, Michael bent over and scooped up Lewis and carried him to the podium.

Said a radiant Jackson to the screaming approval of the fans, "Again I'm deeply moved, and I really appreciate it, and the girls in the balcony, I love you, you're wonderful." To which the girls screamed even louder. Michael continued, "An important chemistry in writing a song is inspiration, and I'm holding one of my inspirations, Emmanuel Lewis!" Giving the V for Victory sign with his left hand, Michael finally looked as if he was genuinely enjoying the evening. Up to this point, he seemed to be acting uncomfortable from all the adulation.

After Willie Nelson was named Favorite Country Male

Vocalist, Michael took his eighth trophy of the evening, for Pop/Rock Male Vocalist. The other nominees were David Bowie, Billy Joel, and Lionel Richie. As Michael accepted this final award of the evening, Diana Ross, who had thrown a fur coat over her gold lamé dress, appeared to congratulate Michael again.

Without a doubt, Michael Jackson was *the* star of the evening. He captured 39 percent of the awards that night, which previewed what was to happen a month later at the Grammys. Especially impressive was Michael's receiving the Award of Merit. At the age of twenty-five he was the eleventh winner, joining a distinguished line of recipients: Bing Crosby, Berry Gordy, Jr., Irving Berlin, Johnny Cash, Ella Fitzgerald, Perry Como, Benny Goodman, Chuck Berry, Stevie Wonder, and Kenny Rogers.

The show itself was viewed by 60 million people, the majority of whom were Michael Jackson fans. The next day every major newspaper in the country was heralding Michael's across-the-board triumph at the American Music Awards. However, the month had just begun, and Michael's mega-press coverage had yet to peak. It was only Monday, January 16, and a week later, on Tuesday, January 24, Michael was scheduled to go before the cameras to film two television commercials for Pepsi—an event that would become front-page news!

CHAPTER FOUR

MICHAEL'S PEPSI COMMERCIALS

Tuesday, January 24, 1984, was a bright, sunny day in Los Angeles, California. The air was warm, the skies were clear and blue. In fact, it was the type of perfectly lit day that had coaxed the movie industry from the East Coast to Hollywood in the 1920s—ideal for capturing images on film under natural sunlight. It was under such perfect conditions that Michael Jackson and his brothers began filming the first of their two historic television commercials for Pepsi-Cola at Burbank Studios, using one of the same city street sets that was used for filming the movie musical *Annie*.

The first commercial involved the interaction between the Jacksons and a group of young kids imitating Michael and his brothers. Michael and representatives of Pepsi reworked the lyrics of his number-one hit "Billie Jean" to become the musical soundtrack for both of the ads and a series of radio spots as well. Also cast in the first commercial was twelve-year-old Alfonso Ribeiro, star of the Broadway show *The Tap Dance Kid*.

Tuesday and Wednesday of that week were used for the filming of the first commercial, and Thursday and Friday were used for the second commercial, which was shot in an indoor concert setting. The shooting was going smoothly, with Bob Giraldi directing and Michael Peters working out the choreography. Until about six P.M. on Friday, that is, when what is now termed "the accident" took place.

Over the next week the news media were filled with shocking accounts of what exactly occurred during that fateful final film sequence. The facts, as chronicled in print, are as follows.

In the Sunday, January 29, 1984, issue of the *Detroit Free Press*, Jeff Hasen reported the following story over the UPI newswire:

> LOS ANGELES—Superstar Michael Jackson, hospitalized with burns from fireworks that ignited his hair during filming of a commercial, was discharged from a hospital Saturday against his doctor's advice.
>
> Jackson's tour manager said the singer requested that a tape of the accident be made public as soon as the film can be processed. "Michael wants to make certain that his fans know exactly what happened," Larry Larson told reporters at the hospital.
>
> Dr. Steve Hoefflin said he believed it was best for Jackson to stay at Brotman Memorial Hospital but reluctantly agreed to his release at 3:30 P.M. Detroit time. Hours earlier, he had told reporters Jackson would be hospitalized for several days.
>
> "We recommended that Michael stay, but we determined this could be done as well out of the hospital as in the hospital," Hoefflin said. "Despite our recommendation, he felt he did want to be treated as an outpatient.
>
> "He was quite happy. He felt better after a good night's sleep. He's in excellent health and was showing very rapid signs of recovery. He's very pleased it was not more of a severe burn."
>
> Jackson, 25, was dancing down a stairway at the Shrine Auditorium on Friday night in a scene for a

multimillion-dollar Pepsi commercial when a special effects smoke bomb apparently misfired and set his pomade-slicked hair ablaze.

At the scene of the accident, the first person to reach Michael after his hair began to burn was Miko Brando, who is a friend of Michael's, and actor Marlon Brando's son. As reported in the February 11, 1984, issue of *Cash Box* magazine, Miko Brando made the following statement at a press conference on February 1 in Los Angeles at the offices of CBS:

There have been many rumors about Michael Jackson's injuries, and some of them are very untrue. I wanted everyone to know the truth and so I asked Michael's lawyer to help me distribute this message to the media.

I was with Michael Jackson all that Friday and was the first person to reach him when he was on fire.

Every previous take of the scene which resulted in Michael's injuries went smoothly. But the final take was very different.

First, as anyone there that day can tell you, the explosion was much larger. It was louder and brighter than any of the other explosions had been.

Also, the explosion was set off sooner than ever before. I watched every take and on the last take Michael had no time to move away from the explosion. He told me yesterday that he was directed by Bob Giraldi in the final take to remain alongside the fireworks until after the explosion, and not to go down the stairs right away like he had in all the other takes. Michael said that the film that he and his lawyer have studied shows this all very clearly.

Michael also told me that he didn't have any oil or hairspray on his hair. His hair was sprayed with water, which probably kept the fire from spreading and causing even more injury.

Michael is feeling better and wanted me to thank all of his fans and friends for the concern and love they have shown.

As part of its Michael Jackson cover story on February 13, 1984, *People* magazine added of the injury:

The fire had scorched a palm-sized second-degree burn on his crown which surrounded a third-degree burn about the size of the hole in a 45-rpm record. An antiseptic cream (silver sulfadiazine) was applied, and Jackson was offered a painkiller, which he at first refused because of his disdain for narcotics. He later accepted an analgesic.

The February 1, 1984, issue of *Variety* reported:

Burns were limited to a palm-sized area on Jackson's pate and hospital spokesman said they had no effect on his face. It will take several weeks to determine the extent of hair loss, but doctors are confident the hair lost will grow back completely— possibly over a several-month period.

One of the biggest concerns, after it was ascertained that Michael would indeed be all right, was the question of whether or not he would be able to attend the megaparty that was planned for February 7 at New York City's American Museum of Natural History—in the elephant room. The day of the party *New York Post* gossip columnist Cindy Adams turned in the following item about Michael's recuperation and status:

Never, not for one moment, was there a possibility that Michael Jackson would blow his party tonight at the Museum of Natural History. His recovery was aided by daily phone calls from Liza Minnelli and Brooke Shields.

In spite of the accident, there was ample filmed footage to successfully complete the second commercial without any problems. The four-day shoot yielded the most famous two television commercials in the history of Madison Avenue—and without a doubt the most dramatically anticipated sixty-second advertising spots ever created!

It was originally planned that both ads would debut on Tuesday, February 28, 1984, during the telecast of the Twenty-sixth Annual Grammy Awards. That promise was upheld on broadcast television, but the night before, cable subscribers to MTV received a special sneak preview of both one-minute spots prior to the Grammys.

As MTV's first half-hour *Monday Night Special*, the acclaimed rock and roll video network presented a documentary about Bob Giraldi's involvement in videos, with the Jacksons, and in the controversial Pepsi ads. The show, which featured footage of Michael's Giraldi-directed "Beat It" and "Say, Say, Say" videos, was capped off with both of the completed Pepsi commercials. The next night the "debut" broadcast of the two ads went as planned, much to the delight of Michael Jackson fans around the world.

Interviewed on the air by MTV's vice president of programming, Les Garland, Bob Giraldi spoke publicly for the first time about the ads, the filming, and the accident.

With regard to the controversial concert commercial, Giraldi explained to MTV viewers, "The story line of the concert commercial is that the Jacksons are at a concert attended by about five thousand screaming, idolizing young kids. We had a live audience of five thousand people approximately. The accident is really something that I can't talk about too much, obviously, because it's very highly technical, and still in the minds of people for a lot of reasons, and I won't talk about it."

"I could tell you what I saw, 'cause it's an experience that brought together a lot of people that tried to help," continued Giraldi of his control-room observations that evening. "Michael was supposed to go, and did go to the top of the stairs. The Jacksons run out on stage, and there's a short dramatic entrance for Michael to come downstairs and to join his brothers, and singing the final lyrics of the Pepsi song, and five thousand screaming young people adore that. Now, I have five cameras going at that, because you can't do that many times, and there's a lot of things to film. And I was in the wings stage right of the setting, and I had five black-and-white monitors that reflect the cameras that I have. And we had done some takes in the morning, and we had done some takes in the afternoon, and it's been reported that this was the last take; and that's just dramatic, it wasn't supposed to be the last take. Michael was situated up there, and I saw him dance down the stairs. And in the black-and-white monitor, I could not tell that his hair caught fire, and it wasn't until I saw everybody rush him on the black-and-white monitors that I knew something was wrong. I thought somebody had maybe come from the stage, out from the audience the way a lot of people do sometimes. And his bodyguards and people ran out, and then they said that his hair caught fire, and we ran out. But there was terrific control. The audience did not go crazy; they were obviously concerned for Michael. Michael was very brave. The film later has shown me that his hair caught on fire, and he came down [the steps] and he was trying to get his jacket off, so I think he thought that it was initially his jacket on fire. And only because he is so incredibly talented, he did two quick spins, and the fire seemed to go out by his own force. Now that film—obviously for the protection of everybody, a case like this is a case that nobody likes to talk about."

Adding to the details of that same shooting, Bob Giraldi also recounted a humorous episode that occurred before the accident. Apparently before Michael's hair was set aflame, another mishap occurred. During a break in the shooting, Michael dropped his white sequined glove into a dressing room toilet seconds before he was to flush! Thanks to soap, water, and a hairdryer, the glove was revived to go on to its present film immortality. Said Giraldi of the comic episode, "He was in my dressing room getting ready with some of the brothers to go on to do one of the scenes, and we were saying, 'Come on, Michael, let's go, we're late.' And he was all dressed up in his wonderful outfit; the same outfit that he wore in the wonderful Motown special. And he said, 'Wait a minute, I have to go to the bathroom. I'll be right with you.' So we're okay, so we waited. And he went into my bathroom, closed the door: 'Ahhhhhhhhhhh!'" Giraldi imitated a startled scream from the bathroom. "And we all are heartfelt, we thought maybe some groupie had kind of like stowed away in the bathroom. We ran to the bathroom, and opened it up, and the fact of what he did was dropped the glove into the toilet! And we all went around crazy, looking for a hanger, and it was Michael who looked at us and picked up the glove himself"—Giraldi laughed—"and it was wonderful! And we cleaned it off and the glove went on to be famous!"

Both commercials have gone on to become advertising classics and have the added unique distinction of being the first TV commercials ever to be listed in the TV schedules of newspapers across America.

To fulfill my further interest in the Jacksons/Pepsi-Cola connection, on April 23 I met with a spokesman for Pepsi, Ken Ross, who holds the title of manager of news media relations. Meeting for drinks at New York City's Grand Hyatt Hotel, Ken filled me in on Pepsi's involvement with Michael Jackson, the Jackson Family, Don King, the TV commercials, and the 1984 Victory tour sponsored by Pepsi. In addition to that, Ken had been present on all four days of filming the two commercials. Our conversation was as follows:

MARK: I've read that Pepsi has approximately $50 million invested in this Jackson venture. Is that an accurate figure?

KEN: That is accurate. I can break down that figure for you if you like, to give you a little clearer understanding. Five million dollars represents our initial deal with the Jacksons, comprised of two key elements: our sponsorship of the upcoming

tour, and their appearance in our commercials.
That accounts for five million of it. Two million
dollars is the price tag on the commercials: production costs for those two spots. They are certainly among the highest costing commercials ever,
among the most expensive commercials ever
made. The balance of that $50 million is what
we will be spending this year in media time to
put those two commercials as well as the re-
mainder of our new campaign for Pepsi on the
air. So that, roughly translated, is about $50 mil-
lion riding on this.

MARK: What happened between the press conference in
November and January when the commercials
were shot?

KEN: Well, that was a lot of creative behind-the-scenes
work, coming up with the story lines for the commercials, working out which music would be used.

MARK: Who had input in that—Michael mostly?

KEN: Yes, Michael had a lot of input. Really three
groups: one, Michael, two, B.B.D.O. [Batten,
Barton, Durstine and Osborn], our advertising
agency, and, three, the creative people at Pepsi-
Cola working closely to come up with story lines,
music, things like that.

MARK: Whose idea was it to bring in Bob Giraldi? Was
that a mutual effort?

KEN: It was a natural choice. We were certainly looking
for a contemporary director who had a good feel
for this type of project. We knew of course that
Giraldi had worked with Michael on his videos.

MARK: . . . and had also worked in commercials . . .

KEN: . . . and worked in commercials, and had an outstanding track record in commercials. And it was
a natural choice.

MARK: And you were at the shooting of the commercials.

KEN: Yes.

MARK: Can you give me some behind-the-scenes information? The shooting obviously started in January.

KEN: The shooting started the third week in January.

MARK: What was the first thing to be shot? Was the last thing where the accident took place? Was that the last segment?

KEN: That was the last, that's right. It was a four-day shoot, two days on each commercial. We opened up on the back lot of the Burbank Studios in Burbank on the set that was used to shoot the movie *Annie*. And under glorious blue skies, we spent two wonderful days shooting that spot, which, perhaps I'm too close to it, but there was a magic there at work. Especially between Michael and Alfonso and the rest of the kids. He loves children anyway, and it was very gratifying to watch that, and as a matter of a fact, after we moved from the first to the second commercial, the kids were gone. Michael told me that he missed him.

MARK: He does like to have kids around, doesn't he?

KEN: Yes.

MARK: So that really was noticeable. There's a different feeling to the commercial, then?

KEN: Yes, there was good feeling on the set, especially between the Jackson brothers and the kids. And Alfonso I think is pure magic. He is wonderful, and I think that he has a very big future.

MARK: Oh, I think so too.

KEN: I understand that Michael and he have since become friends, and he's been out to visit him.

MARK: He really does have an affinity for kids, there's no question. The success of my book *Michael!* has forced me to analyze a lot of what is going on, and I have to say again and again that Michael is really Peter Pan. He really doesn't care to grow up.

KEN: There is an element of that to him, but I think

that that is part of his charm. I think that is part of his attraction.

MARK: It is something that he can identify with.

KEN: When you are talking about Michael Jackson, you are talking about someone with universal appeal. You are talking about someone who transcends every barrier: male, female, black, white, young, old. Those barriers are all broken down under his weight, and that is a rare person and a rare talent that's able to do that. Offhand I can't think of anyone who is on the current scene who is able to do that.

MARK: It is amazing, it really is. Not someone like Elvis Presley had that type of innocence that I think Michael has. It's something unique. Well then, moving right along to the second commercial . . .

KEN: That was filmed at the Shrine Auditorium in Los Angeles, where about a month after the shooting he received eight Grammy Awards on that same stage. Both of the commercials featured Michael's hit song "Billie Jean" with reworked Pepsi lyrics. . . . The use of "Billie Jean" was Michael's idea. It was his idea, and of course we were ecstatic at the possibility of using that tune, which was one of the biggest hits of the year, and maybe the best song of the year in my judgment.

MARK: How can you go wrong? It was my favorite song from *Thriller*.

KEN: It's a song that you don't get tired of, and the lyrics were reworked, of course. . . . Michael collaborated on them along with B.B.D.O. people, and Pepsi A&R people, and voilà, you've got the new theme for those two commercials. That pretty much covers the first commercial.

MARK: This all came together very smoothly?

KEN: Yes, it did—two days. Everybody got a beautiful suntan, and it was very nice. And then we moved into an entirely different setting: indoors, bright lights, audience for one day. The first day's shooting on that commercial was the dressing room scenes and the backstage scene. The second day was with five thousand people in the audience.

MARK: When Michael is in a situation like that, filming something like that, is he very accessible, is he very relaxed, or is he secluded? Did you have any contact with him amid shooting?

KEN: Yes, I did and everyone did. He was not inaccessible at all.

MARK: Was there that theatrical feeling of camaraderie like it was a team effort?

KEN: Yes, absolutely. There was a real sense of a team effort on the whole project. Michael was around the whole time, as were the brothers.

MARK: Then the second day of the second commercial, that's when the accident occurred. What exactly did happen, from someone who was there during the whole shooting?

KEN: I was off in the wings, and my view was obstructed. I didn't know what happened until he came off of the stage, and then it became apparent what happened, that he was burned. Exactly how it did happen . . . I don't think anyone really knows.

MARK: Were there a lot of people watching for mishaps? When you have fire on stage, there must have been someone spotting for trouble. What kind of fire regulations are there for this type of situation?

KEN: Well, there wasn't fire on stage.

MARK: Well, fireworks.

KEN: There were fireworks, there were pyrotechnic effects. Actual fire, no. And it was a very unfortunate accident. Of course our first concern as soon as this happened was for Michael's wellbeing. It became apparent very quickly that he wasn't seriously hurt, that he would be okay, and only then did we really think about what our next step would be. As has been documented, that was the final take, and we used one of the previous takes.

MARK: That was the fifth take, wasn't it?

KEN: That's right. And it was, as I say, very unfortunate. We regret deeply that it happened.

MARK: It was really nothing that anyone could foresee.

KEN: No. Every precaution was taken, and it was an accident.

MARK: When that happened, what was Pepsi's standpoint. Was there chaos? "Are we going to get sued?" There was no panic or anything?

KEN: No, there was no panic. Of course, our first reaction, our first concern was for Michael, and we were quickly in touch with the family, and the Pepsi people visited him, and later that night or the next day it became apparent that he wasn't seriously hurt and that he'd be okay. And of course that was our primary concern.

MARK: As far as the summer Jacksons concert tour, what can you say about the significance of this megaevent?

KEN: We fully expect that this will be the single hottest musical event of this summer, perhaps of the last ten summers. To us it will be an event and an involvement of historic magnitude. It has been so far, and I see no reason why it won't continue in that vein.

MARK: That says it!

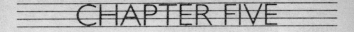

CHAPTER FIVE

OF PARTIES AND PRIZES

It is February 7, and I am standing in the grand foyer of New York City's Metropolitan Museum of Natural History. I am wearing a dark blue tuxedo with a shawl collar, and I am sipping a glass of champagne. Suddenly cannons shoot a blinding blizzard of confetti down on me, and dancers appear on a stage to the beat of a familiar hit record. As the flurry of confetti settles before my eyes, there just six feet in front of me is Michael Jackson. I am at the party of the year!

Neither rain nor snow nor sleet nor hail nor a recently singed scalp could keep Michael Jackson from attending the "Thriller" party that CBS Records threw for him that night. Despite the below-freezing winter temperature in New York City, a crowd of almost a thousand patient fans waited outside the museum that evening for a mere glimpse of Michael. Cordoned off by policemen and police barricades, the fans were lined up across Central Park West, holding up Michael Jackson photos and posters, and waving and cheering at the celebrities who were in attendance.

The invitation to the party itself was one of the cleverest

51

details of the event. It was a single white cloth glove on which was printed:

Walter Yetnikoff
Don Dempsey
Allen Davis

Invite you to a
MICHAEL JACKSON
THRILLER Party
2/7/84   9 PM
AMERICAN MUSEUM OF
NATURAL HISTORY
CPW at 79th St.
Black Tie
RSVP Susan Blond
EPIC Records

You had to present the glove at the front door to be admitted to the party. In fact, you had to show the glove to get anywhere near the front steps of the museum. The glove went on to become one of the hottest Michael Jackson souvenirs of the year (I still have mine safely under lock and key!).

Among the celebrities I ran into that night at Michael's party were Cyndi Lauper, Mary Tyler Moore, Carly Simon, Nicholas Ashford and Valerie Simpson, Nona Hendryx, Peter Max, Joan Jett, Calvin Klein, Andy Warhol, Sean Lennon, Robin Williams, and Gloria Gaynor. For an hour and a half, Michael's 1,500 invited guests drank, mingled, and posed for the many press cameras that flashed in the main hall of the museum as well as in the southern wing filled with stuffed elephants and other animals from the Asian continent.

When the sounds of "Wanna Be Startin' Something" began to pulsate over the powerful sound system in the flower-filled main hall, the crowd sensed that Michael's entrance was near, and everyone pressed in toward the stage.

Dancing in a routine devised and choreographed by Lori Eastside, Michael took the stage as the confetti settled into everyone's drinks and onto everyone's hair. In front of a cheering crowd of acquaintances, well-wishers, and friends, Michael greeted his guests and humbly accepted a host of well-earned accolades.

The first speaker of the evening was Walter Yetnikoff, President of CBS Records. Proclaimed Yetnikoff, "Michael is surely the best artist in the world. Michael just got a presentation for the best solo performer of all time. I'm reading from the *Guinness Book of Records*. The best-selling album of all time is *Saturday Night Fever* with twenty-five million copies globally. I have news for you. Today, we surpassed twenty-five million copies for *Thriller*! Michael Jackson—*the number-one artist in the world!*"

The next speaker was Allen Davis, President of CBS Records International. Said Davis, "Tonight, Michael, your international milestones for the album *Thriller* are a total of sixty-seven gold awards, fifty-eight platinum awards in twenty-eight countries on six continents. And the singles, with nine million sales, have earned fifteen more awards, bringing the total to one hundred forty gold and platinum awards. So far *Thriller* and Michael Jackson have been named Best Artist, Best Male Vocalist, Album of the Year in Japan; Album of the Year, Single of the Year in Australia; Artist of the Year in Italy; Record of the Year in Greece; Album of the Year in Holland; Most Important Foreign Album of the Year in Spain; and International Artist of the Year in Brazil, where the newest dance craze is called 'The Funk Jackson'!"

Michael also received the first edition of the 1984 paperback version of the *Guinness Book of World Records*, presented by its editor and compiler Norris McWhirter. Between January 20 and January 23, the presses were halted so that two new entries could be added to the book at the very last minute, announcing Michael Jackson's *Thriller* as the largest selling album of all time, and as the album with the most top-ten singles (six).

Also, from the stage Walter Yetnikoff read the following letter to Michael:

Dear Michael:

I was pleased to learn that you were not seriously hurt in your recent accident. I know from experience that these things can happen on the set—no matter how much caution is exercised.

All over America, millions of people look up to you as an example. Your deep faith in God and adherence to traditional values are an inspiration to all of us, especially young people searching for something real to believe in.

You've gained quite a number of fans along the road since "I Want You Back," and Nancy and I are among them.

Keep up the good work, Michael. We're very happy for you.

Sincerely,
Ronald Reagan

Good grief! Even the President of the United States was sending Michael fan letters!

Said Michael after receiving all of these honors, "I've always wanted to do great things and achieve many things, but for the first time in my entire career, I feel like I have accomplished something because I'm in the *Guinness Book of World Records*!"

After the presentations, Michael and his date for the evening, Brooke Shields, were whisked off to the room with the stuffed pachyderms, which was blocked off for the use of members of Michael's immediate family. The Jacksons in attendance included Janet, Randy, LaToya, Jackie, Rebbie, Tito, Marlon, and their mother and father. A couple of times during the evening, Michael and Brooke braved the cold February weather to stand on the front steps of the museum and wave to all the fans who enthusiastically awaited a glimpse of their hero.

The night of his party, it was impossible to tell that

Michael had been injured during the filming of the Pepsi commercials only a little over a week before. Michael had a small hairpiece woven into his own hair so that his burn mark was totally invisible to all of us partygoers. Dressed in a pair of jeans, flat black shoes, military jacket, and, of course, a single sequined glove, Michael looked great and seemed in buoyant spirits.

Michael and entourage didn't stay long at the bash, and after posing for a couple of pictures he was whisked away by his bodyguards. However, that was not the end of the party, which cost over $1.4 million and went on into the late hours. I, for one, had a fantastic time, and when I arrived back at my apartment early Wednesday morning, I was still picking confetti out of my hair!

THE GRAMMY AWARDS

The next time I saw Michael Jackson was later that month, in Hollywood. I had flown west to California to throw a party for my first Michael Jackson biography, *Michael!* and to go to the Grammy Awards to watch Michael collect all his trophies. Both the party and my ticket to the Grammys were orchestrated by my dear friend Barbara Shelley. Barbara is as big a Michael Jackson fan as I am, and she decided that it would make for a perfect week of Jackson-mania— and she was right!

On January 10, 1984, I had been invited to the Carnegie Hall Tavern for the official unveiling of the nominees for the year's Grammy Awards. In a room full of other industry insiders, Roberta Flack and jazz instrumentalist Wynton Marsalis read off the nominations. Again Michael Jackson had broken the existing record for most nominations in one year, at a staggering total of twelve!

Michael was nominated for Record of the Year ("Beat It"), Album of the Year (*Thriller*), Best Pop Male Vocal (*Thriller* LP), Best Pop Duet ("The Girl is Mine," with Paul McCartney), Best Rock Male Vocal ("Beat It"), Best R&B

Male Vocal ("Billie Jean"), New Song of the Year ("Beat It" and "Billie Jean"), R&B Song of the Year ("Billie Jean" and "Wanna Be Startin' Something"), Producer of the Year (Michael Jackson and Quincy Jones), and Best Children's Recording (*E.T. The Extra-Terrestrial Storybook*, narration by Michael Jackson).

For me the afternoon and evening of the Grammy Awards was a huge thrill. For years I had faithfully watched the presentation on television, but here I was pulling up in front of the limousine-lined drive of the Los Angeles Shrine Auditorium, prepared to watch Michael Jackson win all his Grammys!

Seconds before the telecast began, a group of bodyguards escorted Michael Jackson, Brooke Shields, and Emmanuel Lewis into their seats, to the screams of delight from the girls in the balcony. Everyone in the orchestra was craning their necks for a glimpse of the superstar "gloved one"! I was in ecstasy as the show began and a star-studded array of legendary hit-makers took the stage.

For this event Michael was clad in another one of his bugle-beaded military jacket creations, this time looking like something President Andrew Jackson would have worn had he become a member of the Supremes. It was a sapphire-blue waistcoat, with the wide lapels lined in light blue bugle beads. Across his chest he wore a matching gold-beaded sash, and on his shoulders were beaded gold epaulets and pads reminiscent of a turn-of-the-century major general. Of course, on his right hand was a white sequined glove, and over his eyes were dark aviator shades. Also on his right arm, Michael wore a sequined tennis sweatband. Swirling gold-beaded braid decorated the forearms of the jacket.

About a half hour into the show, right after Bonnie Tyler sang "Total Eclipse Of the Heart," the first of the Jacksons' Pepsi commercials was viewed in 60 million homes. Right after that, live from London via satellite, outrageous comedienne Joan Rivers and Boy George with Culture Club took the screen to explain the National Academy Recording Arts And Sciences rules. Joan Rivers' monologue was full

It was an exciting afternoon in Manhattan the day that the Jacksons came to town to announce their 1984 Victory tour. (Left to right) MARLON JACKSON, TV star EMMANUEL LEWIS being held by MICHAEL JACKSON, RANDY JACKSON, TITO JACKSON, JACKIE JACKSON, and JERMAINE JACKSON pose with boxing/concert promoter DON KING, who is giving the "V" for Victory at Tavern on the Green, November 30, 1983. (Copyright © 1983 David McGough)

KENNY ROGERS, MICHAEL JACKSON, DIANA ROSS, BARRY MANILOW, and QUINCY JONES at the American Music Awards the night that Michael received the Award of Merit for a lifetime of achievements, January 16, 1984. (*Copyright © 1983 Russell Turiak*)

JERMAINE and MICHAEL JACKSON on stage at L.A.'s Shrine Auditorium filming the controversial Pepsi commercial. This is the moment that Michael's hair caught fire, January 27, 1984. *(AP/Wide World Photos)*

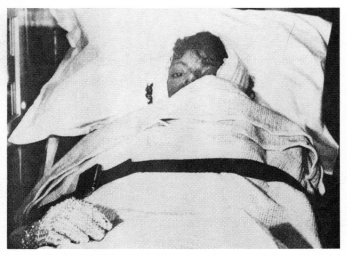

MICHAEL JACKSON is unloaded from the ambulance at Brotman Memorial Hospital after suffering second- and third-degree burns filming the Pepsi commercial, January 27, 1984. Note: He is still wearing his lone sequined glove, which he refused to remove. *(AP/Wide World Photos)*

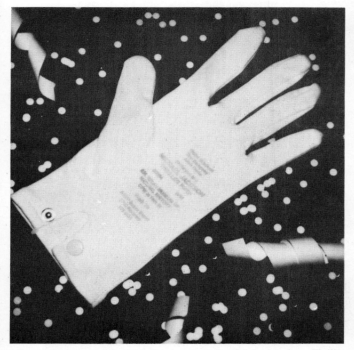
This white glove was the invitation to attend the "Michael Jackson Thriller Party," February 7, 1984. *(Mark Bego)*

MICHAEL JACKSON relaxes in his hotel room hours before he is feted at a Manhattan party in his honor, February 7, 1984. *(Copyright © 1984 David McGough)*

Confetti covered everything as MICHAEL JACKSON made his entrance at his megaparty at New York City's American Museum of Natural History, February 7, 1984. *(AP/Wide World Photos)*

Despite the burns he suffered only a week and a half before, MICHAEL wasn't about to miss the huge congratulatory party thrown in his honor in New York City, February 7, 1984. *(AP/Wide World Photos)*

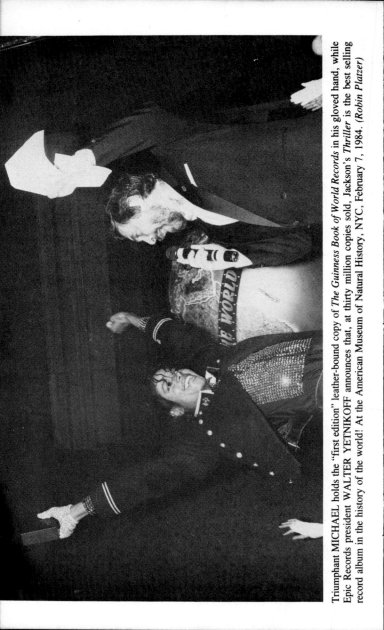

Triumphant MICHAEL holds the "first edition" leather-bound copy of *The Guinness Book of World Records* in his gloved hand, while Epic Records president WALTER YETNIKOFF announces that, at thirty million copies sold, Jackson's *Thriller* is the best selling record album in the history of the world! At the American Museum of Natural History, NYC, February 7, 1984. *(Robin Platzer)*

MICHAEL JACKSON and BROOKE SHIELDS at his "Thriller" party in New York City, February 7, 1984. *(Robin Platzer)*

At the "Thriller" party: RANDY JACKSON, JACKIE JACKSON, MICHAEL, BROOKE SHIELDS, TITO JACKSON, and MARLON JACKSON, February 7, 1984. *(Robin Platzer)*

Twice during the evening of his Manhattan party, MICHAEL went outside to wave to the thousands of fans huddled in the cold awaiting a glimpse of the superstar. To the left is party coordinator STEVE RUBELL, and to the right is his date BROOKE SHIELDS. February 7, 1984. (*Robin Platzer*)

At the unveiling of the Jacksons' Pepsi commercials, ALFONSO RIBEIRO and MICHAEL JACKSON danced on stage at New York City's Lincoln Center reception for Pepsi bottlers, February 27, 1984. *(AP/World Wide Photos)*

MICHAEL cradles his eight Grammy Awards backstage at the telecast, while proud co-producer QUINCY JONES looks on, February 28, 1984. *(AP/Wide World Photos)*

MAUREEN (Rebbie), JANET, and LaTOYA JACKSON join their superstar brother MICHAEL on stage at the 26th Annual Grammy Awards, February 28, 1984. *(AP/Wide World Photos)*

MICHAEL, flanked by members of the singing group MENUDO, shows off his Grammy Awards, February 28, 1984. (John Paschal/Copyright © 1984 David McGough, Inc.)

BROOKE SHIELDS and MICHAEL JACKSON peer out of the window of their limousine the night of the Grammy Awards, February 28, 1984. *(John Paschal/Copyright © 1984 David McGough, Inc.)*

Thumbs up from the world's biggest superstar! After a night of winning eight Grammy Awards, and hopping from one party to another, MICHAEL dropped BROOKE SHIELDS off at her hotel, posed for this shot, and headed for home, February 28, 1984. *(John Paschal/Copyright © 1984 David McGough, Inc.)*

Tiny TV star EMMANUEL LEWIS and MICHAEL JACKSON out for an evening in Los Angeles, March 1984. Those are the leftovers wrapped up like an aluminum dove that Michael is carrying. *(Copyright © 1984 Russell C. Turiak)*

This is the house the Jacksons built! Located in Encino, California, this Tudor-style mansion is where MICHAEL JACKSON lives with his parents and his sisters LaTOYA and JANET. *(R. Eugene Keesee/Photo Trends)*

MICHAEL JACKSON with two close friends: MICKEY and MINNIE MOUSE, at Disneyland in Anaheim, California, April 2, 1984. *(AP/Wide World Photos)*

President RONALD REAGAN and MICHAEL JACKSON at the White House, May 14, 1984. *(AP/Wide World Photos)*

MICHAEL and First Lady NANCY REAGAN share a secret at the White House, May 14, 1984. *(AP/Wide World Photos)*

President RONALD REAGAN presents MICHAEL JACKSON with a Presidential Award for donating "Beat It" for an anti-drunk-driving campaign, while First Lady NANCY REAGAN looks on, May 14, 1984. *(AP/Wide World Photos)*

Author MARK BEGO meets with Michael's sister LaTOYA JACKSON in New York City, April 23, 1984. Here LaToya is showing off the suede fashions that she designed. *(Roger Glazer)*

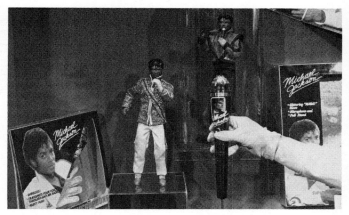

MICHAEL JACKSON merchandising: "The Michael Jackson Doll," "The Michael Jackson Radio Microphone," and of course "The Michael Jackson Glove"! *(Chuck Pulin/Star File)*

The MICHAEL JACKSON Doll! *(Chuck Pulin/Star File)*

From America's *Time* to France's *Paris Match*, MICHAEL JACKSON is 1984's *number-one* cover story! *(Mark Bego)*

Don King received an award from the NAACP in Kansas City, but he also received an edict to "get lost" from Michael Jackson before the tour started. *(Joshua Touster)*

Tito Jackson thanks the NAACP for an award the whole Jackson family received for being an example to the youth of America, and to the world. *(Joshua Touster)*

Michael wears his "award-accepting shades" as he picks up a prize from the NAACP in Kansas City, Missouri. *(Joshua Touster)*

(Joshua Touster)

(Joshua Touster)

Picketing religious members questioned worshipping Michael Jackson. Thousands of "Thriller" fans couldn't have cared less. *(Joshua Touster)*

Jackson-mania hits America! *(Joshua Touster)*

(Joshua Touster)

This portrait of Michael Jackson was sketched by Peter Max, as a gift to author Mark Bego. *(Reproduced with permission from Peter Max)*

of Michael Jackson mentions. At first she announced, "I am thrilled to be on a music show, because I know very little about music. I thought the song 'Say, Say, Say' was Mel Tillis trying to do the national anthem!" She then explained, "I think that the reason we should read the rules is mainly because every one of the nominees out there should know exactly why they lost out to Michael Jackson—okay?!" She then joked to the other nominees, "You shouldn't all think that Michael Jackson is going to get it, because Michael Jackson may not get everything. . . . And just one more thing, though. Just in case, Tito please back up the truck!"

The first of Michael's on-the-air awards was for Producer of the Year along with Quincy Jones. The award was presented by the previous winners of Producer of the Year, the quintet Toto. Quincy spoke first, thanking everyone by name that had anything to do with the album *Thriller*, finishing off with "and Michael Jackson and his beautiful family, and I want to also thank him for co-producing three of the sides on the album, and I think one of the greatest entertainers of the twentieth century—I mean that with all my heart!" Michael then took the microphone and stated shyly with his sunglasses intact, "I don't want to take up much time. I just want to say, Thank you, and I love you all."

After Linda Ronstadt and the Nelson Riddle Orchestra performed, the Beach Boys presented the award for Album of the Year. The nominees were the *Flashdance* original soundtrack, *An Innocent Man* by Billy Joel, *Let's Dance* by David Bowie, *Synchronicity* by the Police, and *Thriller* by Michael Jackson. Accepting the award, Michael introduced Walter Yetnikoff and thanked everyone who had anything to do with *Thriller*'s success. Added Michael, "I'd also like to say something very important; that some people are entertainers, and some people are great entertainers. Some people are followers, and some people make the path and are pioneers. I'd like to say, Jackie Wilson was a wonderful entertainer. He's not with us anymore, but, Jackie, wherever you are, I'd like to say, 'I love you, and thank you so much!'"

After Quincy Jones read off this year's additions to the Grammy Hall of Fame, the second Jacksons Pepsi commercial aired for the first time on network television. From inside the Los Angeles Shrine Auditorium, we members of the live audience viewed it from wide-screen monitors, and we applauded after the controversial sixty-second commercial was over.

Farther into the show, the group Menudo presented the award for Best Children's Recording to Michael Jackson and Quincy Jones for *E.T. The Extra-Terrestrial Storybook*. After Quincy spoke, Michael expressed the feeling that, "Of all the awards I've gotten, I'm most proud of this one...honestly. Because I think children are a great inspiration, and this album is not for children; it's for everyone. And I'm so happy, and I'm so proud, and I'd just like to say, thank you so much!"

After Irene Cara won her Grammy for "Flashdance...What A Feeling," Christine McVie and Bob Seger presented the award for Best Pop Vocal Performance, Male, to Michael Jackson for the album *Thriller*. Accepting this award, Michael invited all three of his sisters, LaToya, Janet, and Rebbie to join him on stage. After joking that his mother was too shy to join him on stage, Michael said, "I'd also like to thank all my brothers whom I love very dearly, including Jermaine!" referring to Jermaine's rejoining the Jacksons for the Victory tour and album. He then thanked Steven Spielberg for the *E.T.* album, and Quincy Jones's wife, Peggy Lipton (formerly of TV's *The Mod Squad*) for helping with *E.T.* as well. Then Michael leaned forward into the microphone and announced, "I made a deal with myself. If I win one more award, which is this award, which is seven, which is a record, I would take off my glasses." The statement elicited screams of joy from the audience. He continued, "Now, I don't want to take them off really. Well, Katharine Hepburn, who is a dear friend of mine, she told me I should, and I'm doing it for her, okay? And the girls in the balcony." At which point he removed his "shades" to the screams and cheers of the audience.

Next Julio Iglesias and Melissa Manchester gave the award for Record of the Year to Michael for "Beat It." It won over Lionel Richie's "All Night Long," the Police's "Every Breath You Take," Irene Cara's "Flashdance . . . What A Feeling," and Michael Sembello's "Maniac." Michael received a backstage congratulatory kiss from Irene Cara and once again took the stage with Quincy Jones.

By accepting this award, Michael set a new record of winning eight Grammy Awards in one year! After taking hold of his final Grammy of the night, Michael said to the cheers of the crowd, "I love all the girls in the balcony! Again, thank you my mother and my father. Thank you Epic Records promotion department, Walter Yetnikoff. Thank the disk jockeys for playing the records. Thanks to the public, I love you all—thank you." After Quincy Jones ran down his list of "thank you's," Michael closed by saying, "I would like to thank Lionel Richie, who is here tonight and is a wonderful person and a wonderful songwriter. I've been knowing him ever since I was ten years old. Also, again Quincy Jones, and the fans in the balcony."

After the awards show I was off to one of the countless parties being held that festive night in Hollywood. The next night I attended the television taping of the first annual Black Gold Awards, produced by Dick Clark. Again my date was Barbara Shelley of Arista Records, and again the winner of the evening was Michael Jackson. Although Michael's parents were there with Janet Jackson, Michael accepted his awards on prerecorded videotape. He was wearing a dark blue sequined top, a wide-brimmed Humphrey Bogart-type hat, and, naturally, his dark glasses. Ruth Robinson of the *Hollywood Reporter* and I laughed that those were his official award-accepting sunglasses!

MAKING AND BREAKING MORE RECORDS

Throughout the first five months of 1984, Michael was consistently represented on the world's record charts. In America, according to *Billboard* magazine, Michael's

Thriller sat at the top of the album chart from the beginning of the year all the way up until the week of April 21, when the *Footloose* (original soundtrack) dislodged it. (However, it continued to remain in the top ten.)

In February 1984 the seventh single was released from the *Thriller* album—the song "Thriller." In *Billboard* the song debuted in the "Hot 100" the week of February 11 at number twenty. The next week the song was number seven with a bullet! Michael had again broken his own record—seven top-ten singles from one album! By June 1984, over 31 million copies of *Thriller* had been sold!

But that wasn't Michael's only appearance on the singles charts. In January a debut single by an unknown artist known as Rockwell was released. It was called "Somebody's Watching Me," and the background vocal was done entirely by Michael Jackson. Rockwell, after initially keeping his identity a secret, was revealed to be Kennedy Gordy, son of the president of Motown Records, Berry Gordy, Jr. The song went on to become a number-one soul hit and a million-selling number-one pop hit as well.

The song "Somebody's Watching Me" is about the paranoia of being watched constantly. The chorus is only seven words: "I always feel that somebody's watching me," but when they're sung by Michael Jackson, it spells h-i-t!

In March I interviewed Rockwell for *Modern Screen* in his room at the Warwick Hotel in New York City. When I asked Rockwell, "How did you end up with the most famous singer in the world singing background on your debut single?" he answered, "Michael? Oh, Michael and I, we're just good friends. We've been friends for years and I've known him since I was young. I'm always interested in what he's doing, and he's always interested in what I'm doing, even though I know more about what he's doing than he knows about what I'm doing.

"But what a perfect person to sing those seven words!" Rockwell exclaimed. "I mean, he's great, he's perfect! If anyone feels that way [watched constantly], he does! He called me up one day, and I hadn't seen him in a long time, and he said, 'Come over. Me and my brothers are working on our album, and we want to see you.' And so he said, 'What are you doing?' So I played him 'Somebody's Watching Me,' and he just flipped. Jermaine and Randy were there, and they loved it too!" And the result is musical history, with Rockwell's album going gold as well!

The next Michael Jackson duet to hit the radio airwaves was "Tell Me I'm Not Dreaming (Too Good To Be True)" from Jermaine's first Arista album *Jermaine Jackson*. The song is great, but there was a bit of a snag connected with it. Epic Records would not give Arista a release to make the Michael-Jermaine cut into a single, so frustrated Jackson fans simply bought the album, making *Jermaine Jackson* certified gold in three weeks from its release in April.

In May 1984, anxious to capitalize on the Michael Jackson craze that was sweeping the world, Motown Records released two Michael Jackson albums, even though he hadn't been on that label since 1976. The first album is called *Michael Jackson And The Jackson Five: 14 Greatest Hits*. The disk is mainly a product of recycled packaging, being a "picture disk" with three caricatures of Michael on one side, and a picture of the early 1970s Jackson Five pressed in between clear vinyl. There are seven solo and group performances on each side, but the real gimmick to end them all is a white glove with "Motown" and "J5" printed all over it in gold glitter. Also enclosed is a badly art-directed collage poster composed of early 1970s Jackson Five photos. Naturally, I bought one for my collection!

Also released at this time was the album *Farewell My Summer Love* and the single of the same name. According to the liner notes, in the early 1970s, when Motown Records moved its headquarters from Detroit to Hollywood, several boxes of unreleased recorded song masters were misplaced. Several songs that Michael Jackson had recorded in 1973 with various producers were recently located, remixed, and overdubbed into this nine-song LP. The three best songs on the album are the title cut, "Farewell My Summer Love," which is a light medium-tempo ballad, the heartfelt "To

Make My Father Proud" with a children's chorus backing him, and the song "Melodie," which was also recorded in 1973 by the Supremes and the Four Tops. Smokey Robinson's "You've Really Got A Hold On Me" gets a fair going over as well, but the material was largely mediocre.

MICHAEL GOES "DISNEY"

Not only is Michael having Disneyland redecorate his home by having the ride "Pirates of the Caribbean" installed in his mansion, but he is expanding the "Michael Jackson Suite" at Florida's Disney World Hotel to accommodate 1984's eight American Music Awards, eight Grammy Awards, four Black Gold Awards, and his People's Choice, and Guinness Book of World Records Awards. According to Michael, "I'm honored to share what is mine with the world. I am here for the people, and what better place to display my personal memorabilia, which is so special to me, than Disney World, where children of all ages can share my joy and deep appreciation."

Up until this recent redecoration, the suite housed thirty-seven of Michael's gold and platinum records and a number of other trophies and awards. The price of staying in the suite per night as of June 1984 is $280 for one bedroom and parlor, and $420 for two bedrooms, as the suite itself is expandable. Talk about the ultimate evening for every Michael Jackson fan! These new additions were announced in March, right after Michael had finished sweeping all of the awards shows.

MICHAEL'S SCALP SURGERY

On Tuesday, April 17, Michael Jackson checked into Brotman Medical Center for surgery on his scarred scalp, resulting from his accidental burn while filming the Pepsi commercial in January. On the next day Michael underwent eighty minutes of revolutionary laser surgery. The use of a carbon dioxide laser meant that there was no loss of blood. Plastic surgeon Dr. Steven Hoefflin used the laser to remove a palm-sized burn from the back of Michael's head and was able to stitch the wound without needing to transplant or implant any new hair follicles from other parts of Michael's scalp.

Hoefflin stated right after the surgery: "Michael is doing fine. We were able to cover the area using his own hair. He did not need any implants or transplants. He really needs to rest, and this will provide him with that opportunity. He jumps back very rapidly, but we would like him to stay here several days. This has been quite traumatic physically and emotionally for him." Hoefflin also said, "The operation was very important to him, to have a full head of hair without the necessity of wigs or other hair coverings. He wanted to get it over with."

MICHAEL JACKSON: MOVER AND SHAKER

In its May 14, 1984, issue, the highly conservative and financially oriented magazine *U.S. News & World Report* published its cover story "11th Annual Survey: Who Runs America." In it they tallied the most powerful and influential movers and shakers in the United States. In the list the "20 Most Influential People Outside Government," they included, #1, Dan Rather (TV newscaster for CBS); #2, Lee Iacocca (president of Chrysler Corporation); #3, Laine Kirkland (union leader of the AFL-CIO); #4, Arthur Sulzberger (*New York Times* publisher); #5, Katharine Graham (*Washington Post* chairman); #6, Jerry Falwell (Moral Majority leader); #7, Jesse Jackson (presidential contender); #8 Billy Graham (religious leader); #9, Roone Arledge (president of ABC News and Sports); and #10, MICHAEL JACKSON! Even David Rockefeller and Henry Kissinger ranked lower than Michael!

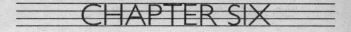

CHAPTER SIX

THE JACKSONS PREPARE FOR THE VICTORY TOUR

From the time of the first of his two 1983 cover stories in *Rolling Stone* magazine, Michael Jackson flatly refused to grant any press interviews. With the exception of his award acceptance speeches and the presentation at his February 1984 party, he remained mysteriously inaccessible. I feel that Michael's total silence, in the face of his enormous popularity, has only intensified his already magnetic appeal. The more he has guarded the enigma of his personality, the more the public's interest, curiosity, and fascination has increased.

As anticipation of the Victory tour drew closer, the other members of Michael's family served as spokesmen for the Jackson camp. Speaking on their roles on the upcoming album and tour, Michael's brothers made various statements, and sister LaToya freely spoke of Michael and of her upcoming third album and fashion line. Here are some of the facts and issues discussed by the Jacksons in the spring of 1984.

MARLON JACKSON

On the Victory tour, each of the brothers is in charge of a different aspect of the stage show. Marlon Jackson is responsible for all the onstage pyrotechnics, or as Jackie puts it, "He's in charge of blowing up stuff!"

Marlon has also been very involved with the group's intricate choreography, and has been responsible for much of it since 1970 when he was thirteen years old. Marlon and Michael come up with the group movements and synchronization, with a little assistance from older brother Jackie. According to Marlon, "We get into a room and listen to the music and come up with ideas."

In 1983 Marlon produced an album for singer Betty Wright titled *Wright Back At You* and sang a duet with her on the LP. There has been talk about Marlon making his dramatic film debut after the 1984 tour, in a Universal film called *Cat*, which may co-star Janet and LaToya Jackson.

In his spare time, Marlon works in his home studio writing songs. For the *Victory* album, Marlon produced, wrote, sang lead vocals, and played keyboards on the song "Body."

Of the then upcoming tour, Marlon commented on all the frenzied activity that was required to have the *Victory* album completed and the stage show in order. According to him, "We seem to have meetings every day. It really gets hectic. We listen to presentations and talk among ourselves. On top of that, I've been spending as much as twelve hours a day in the studio lately getting the album ready."

Explained Marlon, "Put yourself in my situation: I've been doing this since I was six. We've toured our whole lives, and it comes to the point where we said, 'This is getting old. Let's try something new.' But, by us not touring very often, it doesn't mean that we've broken up, that Michael came back to do one tour and then he's going to leave the group. That's *not* the way it is. Jermaine hasn't toured with us in nine years, but Michael has always been a part of the group. You read articles that say Michael doesn't want to tour. He doesn't have to tour. He knows that."

Wanting to set the record straight with reference to their father, Joseph Jackson, and their business dealings with him, Marlon added, "You might also have read that Michael Jackson and the Jacksons fired their father, told him to 'beat it'! That's not true either. My father had a five-year contract with us, which we renewed for seven years. The contract just expired, and we decided not to renew it. It's not that he's done anything wrong. It's just that we needed breathing room. Being in the business with your parents is a touchy thing. To disagree with your father: touchy! So the way we got out of it was to not renew his contract."

Commenting on Michael's *Thriller* album and its vast success, Marlon admitted, "The family had the feeling that it would sell. After all, *Off The Wall* had done eight million [copies sold], so we figured he would at least match that."

Will *Victory* sell the 30 million copies that *Thriller* did? And how much competitive pressure does that apply to the Jacksons? Prognosticated Marlon, "Three years ago it was hard to sell a million, so you can't suddenly expect to sell thirty million every time out. People just don't have the money to support that again so soon. But I do feel that since our last [studio] album [*Triumph*] did about two and a half million, we'll do well over that!"

RANDY JACKSON

When the Jackson Five left Motown Records in the beginning of 1976, Jermaine Jackson made his decision to stay with Motown Records, and youngest Jackson brother Randy joined his other brothers, moved to Epic Records, and began recording with them as The Jacksons. Before that time, Randy performed with his brothers live on stage, so his transition into the quintet was a gradual and very natural one.

One of the biggest records in Jackson history is the song

"Shake Your Body (Down To The Ground)," which was written by Randy and Michael. It went on to sell two million copies. Recalled Randy of the evolution of that song, "I was playing a part of a tune and singing a few words at Havenhurst Studio in L.A. Michael walked into the room and began singing with me. We played and sang it over and over until we had a whole song."

It was a similar situation when Randy was assembling the composition for *Victory* titled "The Hurt." Randy said, "I'd been playing one concept on the keyboards for days at David Paich's house with the drum machine going. One day Michael started singing to it, Jackie joined in, and we worked it until it became a song!"

Randy added, "We've all written and recorded two or three songs for *Victory*. All together we'll have about seventeen songs, but only eight will make it onto the album. The final selections will be made at a family listening party where we'll all vote on the material."

Continued Randy of his job with the Victory tour, "I help select the musicians that tour with us. Then while Marlon, Tito, Jackie, and Michael are working on their parts of the show, I'll work with the musicians and the crew, the guitar tech, the drum tech, and the sound guys. I go to every sound check and check out every microphone. Sound is real important to me. I feel a show can be visually spectacular, but it has to *sound good*! We try to give something special to people. We want them to get more than their money's worth.

"I haven't touched my bass or guitar since synthesizers came out," Randy said. "I'll play bass and guitar on the tour, but in the studio I play keyboards: DX7, Fairlight, DS1, and an Emulator.

"My favorite music is classical: Chopin, Bach, and Stravinsky—especially Chopin," revealed Randy. "When I'm not performing, I'm reading or playing my piano all night long. I like the beach and bicycling."

JERMAINE JACKSON

"We never had really been together and shown what we could do since the Jackson Five," explained Jermaine Jackson of the hot new album *Victory*, which marks the first time that all six Jackson brothers have united on a record since their days at Motown Records in the early 1970s. "It came out really well," he added of the finished product. "We had that special magic to our harmonies. I'm excited because working together is something I've waited for for nine years."

It hadn't been since 1974's *Dancing Machine* album at Motown that Jermaine had been in a studio with Michael, Marlon, Jackie, and Tito. At that time youngest brother Randy was not recording with his brothers, so *Victory* is indeed a unique venture for the guys. In 1976, when Michael and the rest of the brothers went on to Epic Records to become known as The Jacksons, it was Jermaine who stayed behind at Motown to pursue a solo career. The previous year had seen Jermaine wed to Hazel Gordy, the daughter of Motown Records President Berry Gordy, Jr., so his allegiances were divided, and Motown won out on his list of priorities.

In his years as a solo artist at Motown, Jermaine recorded seven albums, most notably *Let's Get Serious*, with the title song written and produced by superstar Stevie Wonder. The record went on to sell over a million copies, and it was nominated for a Grammy Award in 1981.

Just in time for the historic reunion tour with his brothers, he signed with Arista Records and released his label debut album, *Jermaine Jackson*, and never in his solo career has he sounded better. From the dramatic duet that he does on the album with his superstar brother, Michael—"Tell Me I'm Not Dreamin' (Too Good To Be True)"—to the sizzling cut "Dynamite," to the science-fiction-based "Escape From The Planet Of The Ant Men," Jermaine has a surefire hit with the album.

Looking back on his days with the Jackson Five, Jermaine recently recalled, "Michael and I used to sing duets when we used to do club performances in Gary, Indiana. He was five and I was eight. My father had us singing tunes by the Temptations and James Brown. We became so well known that Mayor Richard Hatcher of Gary asked us to perform at one of his functions. Diana Ross was his guest. She saw the show and made a phone call to Berry Gordy. So we auditioned for him at a big mansion in Detroit. I'd never seen a house anything like it. It was so big that he had room for a twelve-hole golf course in the backyard and a bowling alley in the basement. He told us if we got a hole in one, he'd give us $10,000! We were chopping up the course, tearing up the green trying to win that money!"

How does Jermaine feel about seeing old videotapes and listening to records of the Jackson Five? He confessed, "When I look back on the Jackson Five now, it seems like other kids—we're older and different people."

Continued Jermaine of his personal life, "I've been married for ten years to Berry Gordy's daughter. We met in Detroit in 1968 when we were recording the *Diana Ross Presents The Jackson Five* LP. I was thirteen or fourteen years old. Hazel was at the studio with her father; she was thirteen. Now she helps me with business and we write songs together. A strong family is the foundation. When you have success and when you're unhappy, you have to have someone to share it with."

For quite some time, Jermaine worked at Motown Records not only tending to his own career, but looking for new acts to sign to the label as well. Explained Jermaine, "Hazel and I brought DeBarge, Stephanie Mills, and Switch to Motown. I had seen Stephanie Mills in *The Wiz* in New York and signed her to Motown. Then I was in an elevator at Motown in L.A. when Switch handed me a tape. I listened and liked it. So Hazel and I brought them out to L.A., found them a place to stay, and helped them with their act for a few weeks. We set up a showcase with Berry Gordy, and he signed them."

He continued, "I'd met Eldra, the lead singer of DeBarge, in Detroit when I was on a promo tour. He'd been singing gospel and didn't want to leave the church. I envisioned him doing a lot of Frankie Lyman-style songs. Hazel and I got DeBarge out of their contract with a small gospel label and into Motown."

After being at Motown Records for fifteen years, Jermaine felt that he was stagnating, and in 1983 made the decision to leave Motown Records, even though his contract with that label obligated him for more albums. Explained Jermaine of the sticky situation of mixing career and family, "I wanted to have the freedom to keep scouting talent, but it was rough politically to keep doing it at Motown. So I decided to move to Arista. Berry Gordy let me go because he wanted me to be happy."

However, Jermaine still plans to scout for and develop other acts. Even while on the Victory tour, according to Jermaine, "I'll be taking a video camera out on the road to catch new talent while we're touring."

Jermaine has very definite feelings about the immortality of true creativity. He feels that certain songs, movies, and creations are destined to become timeless. He recently recalled one particular conversation he had with Michael about this subject. Jermaine recounted, "Michael and I got into a debate about *Gandhi* and *E.T.* that shows you the difference between us. He's into the magical world and loved *E.T.*, but I felt that *Gandhi* would last longer as a classic because the public could feel that it was about something real. It's the difference between 'Dancing Machine' and 'Never Can Say Goodbye.' 'Never Can Say Goodbye' will be around long after 'Dancing Machine' is gone because it's about real feelings."

One of the most poignant songs on the album *Jermaine Jackson* is the cut titled "Oh Mother," which was written as a salute to his mom, Katherine Jackson. Said Jermaine of her, "Our mother is like E. F. Hutton [referring to the company's advertising slogan]. When she speaks . . . we listen!"

There has been all sorts of controversy in the Jackson camp about family members' dissatisfaction with the involvement of Don King. On that subject, Jermaine explained that the key word in King's pitch to the Jacksons was "family." Said Jermaine, "What we loved about Don King was the fact that he was bringing the family back together— including my mother and my father!"

As you can see, Jermaine Jackson is totally ready to take his solo career to new heights with the new family album, family tour, and his new record label and smash album. Like his biggest Motown hit, "Let's Get Serious," Jermaine is *very* serious about his career and his family.

JACKIE JACKSON

When each of the Jackson brothers was delegated a different responsibility for the Victory tour, oldest brother Jackie Jackson found himself with the task of finding all the professional personnel that the band works with on the road. He's quite an inventive guy and even designed the uniquely special shoes that he wears on stage on the tour. They are Nike running shoes with smooth leather soles so that they can literally glide across the wooden stage without catching on the floorboards the way rubber soles do. To give them the appropriate "flash," they have a luminous stripe that literally glows when he dances onstage!

According to Tito Jackson, Jackie was drafted by the White Sox baseball team when he was nineteen years old, before he started singing professionally. Boasts Tito, "He left training camp and baseball to stay with the brothers!"

Jackie, who enjoys sports like basketball, baseball, and skiing, has been married for nine years, and has two children. His son, Siggy, is seven years old, and his daughter, Brandi, is two.

Looking back on the early days of the Jackson Five, Jackie recalled, "My father played guitar with a lot of semi-pro groups. My mother was singing around the house. She'd sing country and western songs, and we'd harmonize with her. Jermaine had a voice like a twenty-five-year-old. Jermaine and Tito and I started singing at talent shows and started winning trophies. Michael was seven and played congas and imitated James Brown dances!"

One of the most vivid memories of Motown was the audition that the Jackson Five did for Berry Gordy, Jr., at his Detroit mansion. As Jackie remembered it, "We set up our instruments around his indoor swimming pool. Smokey Robinson, the Temptations, and Mary Wells were all there. I was nervous . . . we were singing in front of all our heroes. A week later we were in the studio cutting *Diana Ross Presents The Jackson Five*! The album went platinum!"

TITO JACKSON

On Tito Jackson's wall hangs a plaque engraved with the words "The Gold Ticket Award." It was presented to the Jacksons by New York City's famed Madison Square Garden for selling 140,000 admission tickets between 1970 and 1981. This is a very special award for Tito, because he loves playing for the fans. As he explained, "We go out on tour and knock our cans off for three or four months, and go home for three years and cry because we'd like to be out on the road more." Well, the summer of 1984, Tito Jackson has gotten his wish, and it's being heralded as the biggest tour of the decade!

Tito is thrilled for his brother Michael for all the success he has had with *Thriller*, but is quick to point out that Michael has never left the group that he and his brothers founded so many years ago. Tito said, "Michael is every bit as much a part of the Jacksons as I am. When the six brothers get together and perform, there's something magical that no single brother can project. We have a lot of fun!"

For the *Victory* album, Tito composed the song "We Can Change The World" with Wayne Arnold. Tito wrote the music and most of the lyrics, plays guitar, piano, Moog synthesizer, bass, and is the chief producer on the song. Much of the music on the song was cut in his own twenty-four-track studio, located in the den of his home. Tito said, "My wife is mad because the carpet is in the hall and the sofas are in the entryway. The whole room is filled with recording equipment!"

Tito explained of "We Can Change The World," "The song is about the problems of the world—the fighting, starvation, thieving, children missing from schools, murders—and about people trying to move in the right direction. It has lines like 'All for one is what we should be. If we don't come together, it may all end very soon.' Loving your brother is something a lot of people don't want to give a chance."

According to Tito, on the Victory tour "Marlon, Jermaine, Randy, and I pick the bands, then I teach them the songs and rehearse them. I produced a few cuts for my sister Rebbie, who'll have an LP out on CBS Records this summer. It's a contemporary-rock mixture. I'll travel on this tour with an eight-track studio and write on the road."

He further explained, "I auditioned about twenty guitar players, and Randy auditioned the keyboardist. For the tour we'll carry three guitars: David Williams, Gregg Wright, and myself. Jermaine will play bass, Jonathan Moffett is the drummer, and Randy will handle keyboards, along with two other players."

Commenting on Michael's involvement in the *Victory* LP, Tito said, "Michael has been very, very busy. He's been pulled and tugged here and there by his success, so he hasn't been around as much as he usually is. Sometimes you just have to fill in the gaps, and that's what we've done. We try not to step on each other's toes, which we could easily do. There's a lot of talent in our family: our sisters LaToya and Janet make records, Jermaine puts out records, Michael does, and there are Jacksons records. We try to keep the timing sensible. We had great success with the Jacksons albums, selling platinum records. But Michael's success has been much, much greater. That does keep the rest of us in the shadows. If anything, we help each other because that's the way we were raised: very small houses, lots of children, and Mom and Dad always working. We had to look out for each other. The Jacksons have done a very good job, because a lot of people don't even get platinum records. Michael's success can only help us. He's way up there above us, and maybe he can throw down a rope and let us climb it!

"After all our years in the business, there is still room for us to expand our horizons," predicted Tito. "The year we left Motown, I was set to do my first solo album. Jackie did his there, but I never got around to doing mine. So even if my songs don't make *Victory*, I see myself recording an album and showing my vocal abilities."

Discussing his personal life, Tito explained, "I was married in 1972 and have three kids: Taj, ten, Taryll, eight, and Tito, five. I enjoy working with kids. I've been managing a Little League baseball team for the last five years. We do well, but the most important part of Little League is not winning the games, it's finding the two or three kids who have problems and making them feel like they belong. That's making them winners for life. I find that when you take those few kids and turn them around, you make the team one happy family. Then you win anyway!"

His optimistic feelings about Little League baseball carry over to his feelings about music. As Tito put it, "I love music about what's happening in the world. No one person or ten people can change the world. But if we keep thinking about it, maybe we can do something about it together."

One of Tito's favorite hobbies is working on antique cars. At his house, which is on top of a hill in the San Fernando Valley north of Los Angeles, bodies of quite a few cars in different stages of disassembly await completion. Said Tito, "I restore old cars in my spare time. I started as a kid building go-carts. I'm putting together a 1959 190 SL Mercedes. I have three Model A Fords (one 1929 model, and two 1930 models), and I'm putting together a 1931 Model A now.

Then I have what I call my punk-rock car, a 1957 Edsel. On our last tour in 1981, I carried a magazine that told where in North Carolina you could get a 1930 hubcap and where in Florida you could get a 1929 carburetor. Whenever I could get back to the hotel to the phone, I'd be hunting down the parts I needed."

Continued Tito about his hobbies, "All of us have RV's [recreation vehicles] that we drive up in the mountains. I fly remote control airplanes. Most of them are in pieces— I crash them a lot! I have one with a seven-foot wingspan. And I love to fish!" Well, with the hectic schedule that loomed ahead for the summer, Tito was going to have very little time for fishing. The only hooks that he was bound to encounter were those that lay in the lyrics of the many hit songs that the Jacksons would be performing across America!

LaTOYA JACKSON

On April 24, 1984, with my photographer, Roger Glazer, I directed a fashion layout on LaToya Jackson for *Modern Screen* magazine. After the shooting, LaToya and I spoke about the clothes she designed as part of her new fashion line, her family, and her new album, *Heart Don't Lie*. Having met LaToya a couple of times before when she was promoting her first two albums on Polydor Records, I was pleased to see how her career was progressing in the light of Michael's vast international success. LaToya is lovely enough to be a model, and it has long been anticipated that she would follow in the family's footsteps and become a full-fledged show business entity like Michael and her other brothers.

All her brothers have been very supportive of her solo ventures. Her debut album, *LaToya Jackson*, contained a single called "Night Time Lover" that was produced by Michael and became a chart hit. Her second album was called *My Special Love*. Released in 1981, it featured two cuts produced by Randy Jackson. Her 1984 CBS-distributed album *Heart Don't Lie* (Private I Records) has production work by Tito Jackson, with accompanying singers like the group Musical Youth, and Howard Hewett of Shalamar.

I was pleased that LaToya was stepping out on her own, appearing at the American Music Awards, at the Grammy Awards, and in Michael's "Say, Say, Say" video. Recent interviews in the press have found LaToya admitting that at first she had no desire to join her family in show business. "I didn't want any part of the music business at that time. I didn't like it. Being around it, I began to love it, and I love every minute of it now," she proclaimed.

LaToya feels very protective of her famous younger brother Michael. "He's a very private person . . . very private, and he likes being secluded, away from everyone. He doesn't give interviews. I would say the biggest misconception would probably be the rumor that you hear that he's gay, and it's awful. It's something that we don't like to talk about, we don't care to discuss, because it hurts." Continued LaToya of Michael, "He can't go anywhere, there's always a crowd, but those are some of the disadvantages. With this business come advantages and disadvantages. Everybody in this business—don't let anyone who is singing tell you that they don't want to be where Michael is today, because he's at the top and that's what every artist strives for. They strive to be at the top, and that's where he is, and I think that's what we all want—to see ourselves up there one day."

Of the rumors about her parents separating, LaToya stated this spring, "My parents are still together. They're still at home. And my father, of course he's not signed contractually under Michael, but he does have suggestions, and he puts in, and he tells him what he thinks is right, and they agree on things, and they work things out."

LaToya went on to say that her leather and suede fashions will be available at boutiques around the globe. If everything goes as planned, her personally designed headbands will catch on like the fad Michael started with his single sequined gloves.

CHAPTER SEVEN

MICHAEL JACKSON AT THE WHITE HOUSE

On Monday, May 14, 1984, the President of the United States and Mrs. Reagan, in a magnanimous and unprecedented ceremony, welcomed to the White House a very special guest. No, it wasn't visiting royalty or a reigning monarch, although in his field he is assuredly a crown prince—of pop music, that is. There on the south lawn of the White House was Michael Jackson, dressed in his sparkling blue bugle-beaded Sgt. Pepper-style jacket, a sequined white glove, and his signature dark glasses, accepting a Presidential Safety Communication Award for donating his number-one hit "Beat It" for use in a new public service advertisement warning of the dangers of drinking and driving.

Not often seen in public since his phenomenal ascension to the undisputed throne as the most popular entertainer in the world, Michael was suddenly in the middle of a heavy schedule. Arriving in New York City several days before his Washington, D.C., honors, Michael went into the recording studio to do the vocals for his revolutionary duet with Mick Jagger, "State Of Shock," the first single off the

Victory album. Then on Sunday, May 13, newspapers across the country featured photos of Michael with Shirley MacLaine backstage in her dressing room at the Gershwin Theater, where her Broadway revue was playing. On Monday Michael was off to the nation's capital.

The original idea to use Michael's song "Beat It" for a thirty-second TV spot and a sixty-second radio spot was that of Transportation Secretary Elizabeth Dole. After months of legal negotiations, an agreement was reached with Michael Jackson, and the commercial was produced by the Advertising Council as a public service announcement. It was Dole's plan to have the spots aired at an important time of the year—when many young adults would be attending proms and commencement parties, undoubtedly accompanied by an alcoholic drink or two.

The announcement of Michal's appearance drew a crowd of press representatives (many wearing white gloves!), and outside the tall iron fence that surrounds the White House lawn, hundreds of fans had gathered for a glimpse of the star of the decade. While First Lady Nancy Reagan and Elizabeth Dole looked on, President Reagan, in a witty, punning style, presented Michael with his award.

Said Mr. President, "Well, isn't this a thriller? We haven't seen this many people since we left China! Just think, you all came to see me! No, I know why you're here—to see one of the most talented, most popular, and most exciting superstars in the music world today."

Reagan continued, "At this stage of his career, when it would seem he's achieved everything a musical performer could hope for, Michael Jackson is taking the time to help lead the fight against alcohol and drug abuse. Your success is an American dream come true. Michael, you've made it possible for us to warn millions of young Americans against the dangers of drinking and driving. . . . Thanks to your help, lives will be saved, and no one can put a dollar value on the precious life of one boy or girl. Young people from virtually every family in America will hear these messages on TV and radio."

The President also commended Michael as "proof of what one person can accomplish through a life-style free of alcohol or drug abuse. . . . People young and old respect that, and if Americans can face up to the problem of drinking and driving, we can, in Michael's words, 'beat it.'"

On a light note, Reagan said that many of the White House staff members wanted him to tell Michael to "Please give some T.L.C. [tender loving care] to the P.Y.T.'s [pretty young things]." Explaining with another Jackson song-related pun, he added, "I know that sounds a little 'off the wall,' but you know what I mean." With regard to the then-upcoming Victory tour, the President added, "Michael, I have another message from your fans here. They say they 'want you back,' so when you begin your greatly awaited cross-country tour, will you please be sure to stop off here in the nation's capital?"

Michael, who stood arrow straight behind his dark glasses for the nine-and-a-half-minute ceremony, stepped up to the microphone with shades intact to announce proudly the twelve-word sentence "I'm very honored; thank you very much, Mr. President and Mrs. Reagan."

The award plaque itself read:

PRESIDENTIAL AWARD

MICHAEL JACKSON

To Michael Jackson with appreciation for the outstanding example you have set for the youth of America and the world. Your historic record-breaking achievements and your preeminence in popular music are a tribute to your creativity, dedication and great ability. The generous contribution of your time and talent to the national campaign against teenage drunk driving will help millions of young Americans learn that "Drinking and Driving Can Kill a Friendship."

May 14, 1984   THE WHITE HOUSE

After the reception on the south lawn, Michael was supposed to meet a few children of White House staff members who wanted to say hello. However, when he arrived at the Diplomatic Reception Room, there was a horde of seventy-five star-struck adults. At the sight of the crowd, Michael freaked out and ducked into the men's room off the Presidential Library. After coaxing from some of the officials, Michael was persuaded to greet the children and their parents. Aside from that, the ceremony went without a hitch, and Michael was officially proclaimed a national treasure.

JACKSON MEETS JAGGER

The week of June 10, 1984, radio stations began to unleash onto the airwaves the hottest new Michael Jackson song— his duet with Mick Jagger of the Rolling Stones, along with the Jacksons. Titled "State Of Shock," it was just that for many Jackson fans, as the song's sound is obviously tailored for Jagger. But the second I heard the rousing rocker with various layers of vocal tracks, I knew that it would be a million seller and the official anthem for the summer of 1984. The Thriller and the Rolling Stone had come together in the recording studio and come up with a killer—a shocking, rocking, high-intensity hit with a heavy bass line and an infectiously throbbing tempo. Michael and Mick's vocals literally punctuate the music with attitude and sassy confidence.

A PRISONER IN DISGUISE?

There had been all sorts of talk about Michael Jackson feeling that he couldn't go anywhere in public without bodyguards, and even that was a hassle because as soon as he was recognized, he wouldn't be able to relax and enjoy himself. Every outing turned into an appearance. To alleviate this problem, Michael purchased a $10,000 professional makeup kit from Rick Baker. In mid-May newspapers flashed pictures of Tatum O'Neal with a bearded young man in a bushy Afro attending a Kool and the Gang concert at New York City's Radio City Music Hall. You guessed it! That was Michael!

In April a song titled "Eat It" by "Weird" Al Yankovic hit the top-ten charts. It was a takeoff of Michael's "Beat It" and humorously poked fun at fussy eaters. Weird Al also did a riotous video that was a direct takeoff of Michael's famed video of "Beat It." The last shot shows Weird Al lying in bed suffering from indigestion from having eaten so much. As he leans forward to get some seltzer, we see a close-up of his eyes, and they're identical to the yellow slit cat eyes that Michael has at the end of his "Thriller" video. A very sharp and clever lampoon, indeed!

In May Michael Jackson's lawyers began cracking down on the manufacturers of unofficial Michael Jackson merchandise. Posters, buttons, sunglasses, and T-shirts were among the most prominent ripoffs that proliferated on the marketplace. According to Stephen Huff, Michael's New York lawyer, Jackson "is concerned that the public doesn't get cheap, inferior goods." There was an estimated $50 million in bogus Michael Jackson souvenirs on the marketplace at this time.

SOMETHING'S ROTTEN IN VICTORYVILLE

The first inklings of dissension in the ranks of the Victory tour camp came in February 1984. It was clear to me then that this was a case of too many chiefs, and not enough Indians. Everyone involved wanted the final say, and troublesome stalemates occurred. By mid-June, the megasummer concert tour to end them all, which was supposed to have commenced around May 31, still had no final dates or a single venue contract signed.

My initial suspicions regarding Michael Jackson's trust of Don King were proved accurate in the March 15, 1984, issue of *Rolling Stone*. The original deal had Don King splitting 15 percent of the monies derived from the tour with Joseph and Katherine Jackson, equally. According to the statement by Michael's lawyer John Branca in *Rolling Stone*, "Don King was not Michael's first choice to promote the tour. This tour is important to Michael because it's important to Michael's family. I'm not sure the tour was Michael's first choice. He might have preferred to do other things. But he found it important to tour at his brothers' request and his family's request. They very much wanted to work with Don King. So Michael said, 'If it's that important to my father and my family, I will work with Don King.'"

That same issue of *Rolling Stone* also spoke of a letter to Don King from Michael Jackson. In it King was officially instructed:

   not to communicate with anyone on Michael Jackson's behalf without prior permission;

   that all moneys paid to Michael Jackson for his participation in the tour would be collected by Michael Jackson's personal representatives, not by Don King;

   that King did not have permission to approach any promoters, sponsors or any other persons on Michael's behalf;

   that King was not to hire any personnel, any local promoters, book any halls or, for that matter, do ANYTHING without Michael Jackson's personal approval.

Commented King, "With Michael, you are always on trial." John Branca said, "Unless the tour is handled properly—financially, creatively, and otherwise—Michael is not going to go out.... I worry all the time. The Pepsi incident has caused everybody to be a little concerned. The Who had riots. With a tour of this magnitude, it's got to be planned with perfectionism to make sure it's conducted smoothly."

The first six months of 1984 saw a host of changing

personnel in the Jackson camp. First of all, Michael hired a new personal manager, Frank Dileo, who as vice president of promotion at Epic Records played a key role in *Thriller*'s success. Apart from Michael, the Jacksons signed a new manager as well, Jack Nance. All of these people worked along with tour coordinator Larry Larson.

During the spring, Larson was called by Michael regarding the stage set for the Victory tour. Michael said, "Larry, I have a few ideas for the show." Explained Larson recently, "He recited his whole résumé for the last year. He explained that he'd made videos, that they had all come out pretty well. He was trying to show that he should be taken seriously." Larsen proceeded over to Michael's house to discuss the subject. He admitted later, "I was amazed. He had a pile of storyboards he'd drawn himself . . . storyboards complete with stage sets, costumes, the works! He began to narrate the show that unfolded like a story, illustrating what he was talking about with his drawings. I was astonished! It was fabulous!"

Meanwhile on the tour-scheduling front, confusion reigned. In April it was announced that a New England concert promoter named Frank Russo would be coordinating the dates along with Danny O'Donovan. The pair had guaranteed $40 million to the Jacksons, aiming at a June 22 debut of the concert. Russo apparently spoke too soon and told a reporter from the *Providence Journal*, "He [Don King] has nothing to do with the actual promotion of the tour." King was not amused at seeing this in print and countered, "I won't work with the guy. He said bad things about me." In May, Russo was axed. A statement from the Jacksons in the May 16, 1984, edition of the *Providence Journal* read "Frank Russo's potential relationship with the Jacksons' tour was contingent on his ability to work out an arrangement that everyone on the Jacksons team could live with. Unfortunately, Frank was never able to work out an arrangement of that nature."

Finally, in June the Jacksons signed a contract with Chuck Sullivan and his company, Stadium Management Corporation. Sullivan is executive vice president of the NFL team the New England Patriots. According to Jacksons manager Jack Nance, "Stadium Management Corporation's experience is ideal for this tour. Chuck Sullivan has worked with enormous audiences, frequently under the most difficult conditions. Through his NFL contacts, he can work successfully with the city officials of any community in America. The tour the Jacksons have planned is extraordinarily ambitious and imaginative. And the crowds, we're told, are likely to be the largest the entertainment industry has ever seen. Sullivan's experience organizing spectaculars for enormous audiences will be invaluable to us."

At the time Chuck Sullivan stated, "The Jacksons are the premier musical attraction in the world today. We are thrilled to be able to work with them on the 1984 Victory tour. Joe, Katherine, Don, and I will consult frequently on all of the tour's details."

However, June 10 passed, and there was still nothing definite, only the rumored possibility that the tour would start June 22 in Lexington, Kentucky. Then it was rumored that it would be on June 29 in that same city. It was also rumored that many major cities would be omitted from the itinerary for security reasons. Finally, on Friday, June 15, the first three dates of the Victory tour were announced. At long last the Victory tour was on its way, and I could finally pack my suitcases for the ultimate Michael Jackson adventure!

CHAPTER EIGHT

KANSAS CITY, DALLAS, AND JACKSONVILLE

The first week of July 1984 was truly "Jacksons Week" for me! On Monday, July 2, the *Victory* album was officially released just in time for the first concert in Kansas City, Missouri, that Friday night. Knowing that I was set to leave my New York City apartment behind me for the next three to four months to follow Michael Jackson and his musical family across America, I had dozens of errands to run in Midtown Manhattan.

As I walked up the Avenue of the Americas in the muggy 90-degree heat, trying to remember everything that I was supposed to do that day, I reached the Sam Goody record store near Rockefeller Center. I ran in to see if the long-awaited LP was indeed out, and no sooner had I passed through the revolving glass doors and into the luxuriously cold air of the record store than I saw it! There, three steps up on the landing of the main floor of the store was a floor display filled with *Victory* record albums and tape cassettes.

The display itself was set up like a virtual shrine to Michael and the Jacksons! I immediately purchased one *Victory* album and one *Victory* tape. As I was becoming known as a fervent "Jacksonologist," I knew that I couldn't live another minute without one of each! The latest issue of *Billboard* magazine had already proclaimed "State Of Shock" the "most added" radio single nationally for that week, and I couldn't wait to hear the rest of the album.

The whole beginning of that week I spent deciding exactly what to pack for the Victory tour. Did I really need five different pairs of dark sunglasses? Of course. I couldn't let those fashion-setting Jackson brothers be the only ones on this tour with a full wardrobe of shades!

On Thursday, July 5, as my plane took off from La-Guardia Airport, it was my tape of the *Victory* album that was blasting out of the headphones of my stereo tape player. As "State Of Shock" rang in my ears, the plane left the ground, and at long last I was officially off on the most exciting summer adventure of my life—following the Jacksons to *every* Victory concert!

When I landed that sunny afternoon at Kansas City International Airport, I was met by photographer Josh Touster, who had arrived an hour earlier from Los Angeles. After I reclaimed my luggage from the baggage conveyer belt, I suggested to Josh, "Why don't I call Ken Ross of Pepsi right now, just to check in and see what the schedule of events is?"

"Sounds good," Josh agreed.

After I got Ken on the phone, he announced to me, "You're both invited to a press party and a dinner at Arrowhead Stadium for the Jacksons. It starts at 6:30 P.M."

It was already 5:45 P.M., I hadn't shaved, I was hot and tired, and I had never been to Kansas City in my life. Could we actually make it in time? Of course. If there's a good party going on, I can find it!

I shaved in the bathroom of Hertz car rental, found the stadium, changed my clothes in the parking lot, and arrived just in time for cocktails! And that was typical of the pace of the next ninety-six hours, with the next night being the first of Michael and the Jacksons' Victory concerts!

The party was full of press, media, and public relations friends from all over the country, all psyched up for the debut performance of the concert event of the century. Two hours in town and I was already having a great time!

From that moment on, for the next three days I became just one of over two hundred journalists who had descended upon Kansas City. A local daily newspaper, the *Kansas City Star*, portrayed us for their readers as a pack of scoop-crazy Clark Kents and Lois Lanes by proclaiming in a cover story that "notebooks, cameras, and press badges identified the small army of news hounds roaming the stadium grounds." No description could have been more apt. It was what I call "kamikaze journalism" at its finest: "Dive in there with your notebook and don't come up for air until you have a story!"

After dinner that night, when the Kansas City Chiefs' football cheerleaders—the ultracute Chiefettes—passed out official Pepsi "Victory Tour" T-shirts, I knew what I was dealing with. The T-shirts went quicker than a blue-light special at K mart. They were grabbed so fast you'd think that the Chiefettes were handing out gold!

For Josh and me and the rest of the media pack, Friday morning before the concert began with massive quantities of coffee in the press room of the Crown Center Hotel. It was there that the prized press credentials, tickets, and parking passes were distributed to reporters from all over the world by Beverly Paige and Leah Gramatica of the publicity firm the Howard Bloom Organization, and Susan Blond, the vice president in charge of publicity at the Jacksons' record label, Epic Records. Glen Brunman, of the CBS Records West Coast office, and Ellen Golden, of the Bloom office, were responsible for photo passes, which were even more scarce than press passes. Only fifteen still press photographers were allowed to shoot opening night, and they weren't allowed any closer than the twenty-eighth row of the orchestra, or floor, area of the audience.

That afternoon at 3:30, Michael Jackson and his entire family were to receive an award from the Los Angeles and Beverly Hills-Hollywood branches of the NAACP in the Crown Center Hotel's huge Centennial Room B. Twenty-five members of the press had already begun waiting outside the banquet-sized room when Josh and I got there at 2:30 P.M.

By the time the doors to the room were opened, it was almost 3:30: The first people allowed in the room were camera crews from television networks, all lugging video equipment in the form of power packs, cameras, broadcast microphones, and even stepladders to stand on. Admitted next were still photographers and writers, The setting was a long room with an elevated speaker's dais at the far end. A velvet rope defined in no uncertain terms the closest we news hounds would be allowed near the dais. The scene looked to me like a frenzied Battle of the Tripods as photographers elbowed each other for finer vantage points from which to shoot the gloved superstar. As soon as one line of access was established at the edge of the rope, a line of higher tripods would be set up behind them. One photographer set up his massive tripod, and instead of putting his camera on it, he sat on top of the tripod and held his camera! Other photographers grabbed stray chairs to stand on. This would be the closest that any member of the media would be allowed near Michael Jackson, so the atmosphere was frantic, to say the least!

One of the most prominent video camera crews was a three-man team from NFL (National Football League) Films. They were hired personally by Michael Jackson to capture on film everything that would happen on the Victory tour, obviously for a film, a TV special, and/or a video cassette presentation of the whole tour.

It was 4:30 by the time things got under way. Many high-ranking officials of the NAACP spoke about the importance of the unity of the American family. Then at long last Michael and Tito Jackson took the podium to accept the 1984 Dr. H. Claude Hudson Medal of Freedom Award and the 1984 Olympics Medal of Friendship Award on behalf of the entire Jackson family (Joseph, Katherine, Jackie, Rebbie, Jermaine, LaToya, Tito, Janet, Randy, Marlon, and of course Michael).

Dr. Benjamin Hooks, the executive director of the

NAACP, stated to the crowd, "It is a great honor to be here . . . to have an opportunity to honor this family. . . . For those of you who watched steadily the Jackson children grow up and mature to adulthood, we cannot help but share their pride and thrill of ongoing success. I think all of America ought to be proud of this Jackson family. They are a remarkable family, they are worthy of emulation, they are worthy of being noted, they are worthy of being duplicated and replicated. Their fame has been tremendous, and yet they have retained a certain type of humility. We're proud of the fact that when Michael released that *Thriller* album, it did not deal with kinky sex or drugs or any of those subjects, but was clean, good music and has made a record . . . and we're proud of that. The NAACP is proud today to join with the branches in Los Angeles in presenting the H. Claude Hudson Award. We want the whole world to recognize the Jacksons, not only for their singing ability, but for their dedication and devotion to the ideals of America, for they represent the highest and best aspirations of every little black boy and girl, white boy and girl, anywhere in this country. They can look up to them with pride and admiration, and we want the world to know that, and we want to be part of making that so."

Behind our crowd of eager newsmen and newswomen stood another velvet rope. Behind it stood delegates of the NAACP, many of them with their children. As Michael and Tito appeared, high-pitched screams sounded from the back of the room. Michael was dressed in a brightly beaded silver and white jacket, a bugle-beaded red sash, and his signature dark glasses. A trademark white sequined glove was on his right hand.

Polite and soft-spoken Tito, who was bestowed the honors first, stated to the press and delegates, "I'd like to say thank you very much. This is some type of special award for us. On behalf of myself and my brothers, my mom and dad, sisters, it's good to know that everything we do is positive, and you've shown us the right direction. Thank you very much."

As timid Michael took center stage, the camera-operating men and women shouted out from all directions to catch his attention and get him to look directly into each of their lenses. A cacophony of "*Michael*, look this way!" "*Smile*, Michael!" filled the room. A blinding sea of flashbulbs flared like fireworks as Michael waved his gloved hand at all of us assembled in the closely guarded room. Accepting the framed awards, he stated in a mere fourteen words, "This is a great honor. Thank you very, very much. I love you all."

The mayor of Kansas City, Missouri, Richard L. Berkley, presented Michael with a commemorative book and the key to the city. That was it—a two-hour wait and two minutes of Michael.

Among the other Jackson-oriented news of the day was the announcement that the Hollywood Chamber of Commerce had approved a Michael Jackson star on its celebrated Walk of Fame, to be embedded in the concrete of the sidewalk along Hollywood Boulevard. In the late 1970s there was already a "Jacksons" star dedicated, so this made Michael the first celebrity to have two different stars dedicated to him along the Walk of Fame!

Despite the manic, media-hungry atmosphere, and all the worries about security problems that had plagued the Victory tour before the concerts in Kansas City, opening night went quite smoothly. I've never seen such a polite and orderly crowd of 45,000 in my entire life. Like everyone else who had been following the progress of the Victory tour, my biggest fear was that there would be a total mob scene, with people pushing, shoving, and getting trampled to death. Miraculously, all my fears evaporated that first night at Arrowhead Stadium. After I learned that the stadium itself was located in—are you ready for this?—Jackson County, Missouri, I took it as a favorable omen.

My instincts were quite correct. The audience was very much a family audience, with lots of orderly parents and their children politely filing into their assigned seats. Mellow and subdued was the opening-night audience this Friday in Jackson County, Missouri. I think that on this opening night, neither the audience nor the Jacksons were quite sure what to expect in terms of the outcome of the evening. Everything went very smoothly Friday night despite the intense pressure on the Jacksons to impress, and the intense pressure on the audience to be impressed and have a wild time without anyone getting hurt.

That first night was a total success on all counts—the Jacksons wowed the crowd, and the audience had a well-behaved but emotionally exciting time. There were some obvious bugs to be worked out in the show itself. The mock argument that the brothers had before Jermaine's solo spot was awkwardly written, stagy, unspontaneous, and stiff where it should have been comic. Jermaine's ballad "Do You Like Me" was the unanimously-agreed-upon low point as far as pace and excitement were concerned.

Major criticisms from the fans and the critics were that Michael did not perform his top-ten tribute to monster movies, the eerie and exciting "Thriller," and that the Jacksons did not perform one single song from their brand-new album, *Victory*. How on earth could they have shipped a record amount of two million copies of the *Victory* album on Monday of that week and not introduce a single song from it on Friday?

At a press conference directly following the opening-night performance, Jacksons publicist, Howard Bloom, explained to us reporters that no songs from the new album had been included because the Jacksons were concerned that their fans wouldn't recognize any of the tunes, thus creating a lull in the show. I could see where it would be difficult to do the single "State Of Shock" without Mick Jagger to share the lead vocals with Michael as he does on the record, but I thought that at least the hot dance cut "Torture," which opens the *Victory* album, would have fit perfectly into the show. The excuse given for the obvious omission of the song "Thriller" was that too many religious leaders of Michael's faith, the Jehovah's Witnesses, had complained that it glorified satanic worship, the occult, and evil in general.

Some people have no sense of humor whatsoever!

The show was originally supposed to be two and a half hours long, so when it turned out to be forty-five minutes shorter than that, some people were taken aback. Local promoter Russ Cline took the blame for having publicly announced that the show would be two and a half hours in duration by stating, "When we estimated how much time it would take between songs, we figured it would be longer than it turned out to be. Thus the show was forty-five minutes short." I personally didn't see how Michael's vocal cords or stamina could have accommodated an extra hour of lead singing and dancing each performance. This might have led to his collapsing sometime later in the summer. The show, in my mind, was tight, fast paced, and, quite frankly, all of the spectacular entertainment that it was supposed to be.

The next day the headline in the *Kansas City Times* announced, "And Behold! He'd Off and Singing," in big, bold black type. Reviews from around the country were decidedly mixed, but it would be hard for any show that did less than part the muddy Missouri River to live up to everyone's expectations that night. On Saturday night, from the very first moment that the house lights went down, the excitement level was much higher than the previous evening. The Jacksons were much more loose and at ease, and were obviously enjoying themselves much more. The audience reacted with much louder, more enthusiastic responses, and the evening was altogether more "thrilling"! It was as though the pressure of seeing if the show would actually work before an audience was over, and everyone could get into just enjoying the whole event.

The first two nights, I saw the Kansas City show in elevated areas with other press members and Pepsi guests. On Sunday night I watched it from the floor, or orchestra, level, thanks to my all-access press badge. That third night in Kansas City, I really got into the crowd and the fans, who were clearly getting their money's worth of excitement from the legendary twenty-five-year-old Michael Jackson and the show that he was the star of. On the second and third nights of the concert, there were also marked improvements on stage. Even Jermaine's "Do You Like Me" worked much better.

On opening night there were all sorts of rumors that Diana Ross or Paul McCartney and/or Mick Jagger would attend and possibly appear with their singing partner Michael. In Kansas City the only celebrities in the crowd were Presidential candidate Jesse Jackson on Saturday, and Wayne Newton on Sunday. Neither appeared on stage.

At the post-concert press conference Saturday night, publicist Howard Bloom explained many of the details of the show to us members of the media, including the following facts:

The levitation illusion was designed by Michael and Franz Harary, not magician Doug Henning, as it was rumored.

Michael and his brothers designed the spider monsters, and the blinking eyes of the spiders were actually helicopter searchlights.

The Kreeton people were Michael's design, and he named them with his own spelling in his own handwriting on the original sketches.

Fifteen hundred people were employed per night, 130 who travel with the show from city to city.

There are two stage bases which leapfrog each other from arena to arena. While we looked out of the windows of the press box at the "A" stage at Arrowhead, the "B" stage set was already at Texas Stadium in Dallas, Texas.

Tour manager Chuck Sullivan then informed us that local black promoters would be affiliated with local white stadium managers in each of the future cities, to assure total racial harmony and promotional saturation in each city's local communities. Added Sullivan of the Victory tour, "It is insured for more than most cities in America!"

In Kansas City, Missouri, over 160 law enforcement officers, drawn from four different area police departments, augmented 375 privately-hired security people. Also on hand for safety's sake were nine paramedics, two doctors, six nurses, one emergency helicopter, and four ambulances. There were fortunately no mishaps, but as the old adage goes, "An ounce of prevention is worth a pound of cure"! Also as a precaution against any troublemakers, no one was even allowed in the parking lot of Arrowhead Stadium without producing a concert ticket for that evening. Everyone entering the stadium was also subject to a metal-detector scan, and if need be, a physical frisking.

Official Jackson souvenirs sold briskly at many booths set up on the grounds. T-shirts bearing the Jacksons and/or Michael solo, sold for $13, or $20 for a heavier, sleeveless sweat shirt model. Also for sale were Jacksons buttons ($2), Jacksons bandanas ($6), Jacksons headbands ($5), and Jacksons sunglasses ($12). The *Kansas City Times* estimated that $1.5 million in Jackson memorabilia was sold in this three-day period alone!

Before Sunday night's show in Kansas City, Michael's personal publicist, Norman Winter, informed me that not only was Michael going to donate his own proceeds from the Victory tour to various charities, but he had recently donated funds for a nineteen-bed facility at New York City's famed Mt. Sinai Hospital for leukemia research. Winter also informed me of the compilation record album called *Let's Beat It*, manufactured by the K-Tel label. Michael donated the funds that his songs "Say, Say, Say" and "Human Nature" would earn in publishing and royalties from this album. The money from the sale of the *Let's Beat It* record album would go directly to the T. J. Martell Foundation, which was founded to discover a cure for leukemia.

After opening night in Kansas City, Michael consistently wore black tuxedo pants instead of the black and white vertically striped ones. After that, Michael's wardrobe remained pretty much unchanged, with the exception of replacing his sequined cummerbund with a better fitting one in Jacksonville, Florida, and occasionally sporting a differently styled jacket for the opening number. However, his other brothers varied their outfits on subsequent nights. On the second night in Kansas City, Randy wore the striped black and white pants. The next night Randy wore a white top and tight red spandex pants. Sunday in Kansas City found Marlon in brown harem pants, Tito in a flashy suit of sequined black and white with huge red stars and yellow V-shaped shoulder pads, while Jermaine was in knee-high red boots over black spandex pants with a sequined black and red jacket.

On top of the costume variations, Jermaine also displayed a number of different guitars from his personal collection, including a unique one made of clear lucite on which was mounted a huge sparkling black widow spider on a white web. Another one was shaped like a machine gun. Flash and glitzy showmanship was what the crowds came to Arrowhead Stadium for that sizzling 100-degree weekend in July, and that's exactly what they got!

After seeing all three Jacksons concerts at Arrowhead, I was exhausted. Like the pace of the show itself, the excitement hadn't let up from the minute I got off the jet three days previous. I could just imagine how Michael Jackson felt. During his stay in Missouri, he had snuck out of his room at the Alameda Plaza Hotel to catch two movies: *Gremlins* and *Ghostbusters*. Other than that, he had been busy creating his own brand of supernatural magic on stage for a record crowd of 135,000 fans. That sold-out total topped any previously set record for concert attendance ever performed in Kansas City.

On the following Tuesday, local FM radio station KLSI announced that during the nearly two hours that they spent on stage, the Jacksons had made $1 million per hour and a total of $6 million during their three-day stay. The radio station also estimated that the revenues from hotels, restaurants, and other facilities generated $26 million for the city and its businesses, all due directly to the Jacksons' concerts.

That weekend, from points around the world, all eyes were on Kansas City, Missouri, the Jacksons, and especially Michael Jackson. In spite of a mediocre review or two, the first three dates of the Victory tour were a roaring success, with the show improving in quality and feeling each night. Next stop on the agenda—Texas Stadium near Dallas, Texas.

DALLAS, TEXAS

Missouri may be known as the Show-Me State for its inhabitants' supposed skepticism, but the week that the Jacksons played Dallas, it looked as if Texas had cornered the market on doubt. Of the two daily newspapers in town, the *Dallas Times Herald* took especially great pleasure in setting the scene for a potentially less than enthusiastic reception.

In his opinion-society column, writer Jim Schultze outlined the situation by pointing out that "it was Dallas where the Jackson tour hit sand. Ron Chapman of KVIL has been describing it by saying that 'the Michael Jackson Resistance Movement started in Dallas.'"

On Friday 13, also in the *Dallas Times Herald*, Joe Rhodes wrote on the front page of the "Living" section, "Come on, kids. Get a grip. This Jacksons business has gotten out of hand, hasn't it? . . . Look at yourselves, twitching like marionettes on the end of Don King's string, or Chuck Sullivan's string, or whoever it is that's running this whole Jacksons Victory Tour circus train. . . . I have witnessed the first show of the Jacksons Victory Tour. And—trust me, friends—it wasn't that big a deal. Michael didn't save the whales or stop acid rain or announce that he's really Diana Ross or anything like that. No one came out of their wheelchairs or threw away their canes. Hell, no one even rushed the stage." The majority of the article was continued on page four, placed under a review of the *Victory* album titled "'Victory': A serious letdown."

Adding to the negative atmosphere, only three days before the concerts were to begin, thousands of tickets still remained unsold. Had the tour hit another iceberg in Dallas? Would the hierarchy of the tour screw things up with their all too obvious greed? Were the Dallas dates to become a disastrous fiasco? Both Dallas daily newspapers asked their readers these questions that week.

Well, you know what happened? The first Dallas concert that Friday the thirteenth proved anything but unlucky for the Jacksons as they worked their tails off and gave their absolutely best concert yet! When Eddie Van Halen suddenly appeared on stage to play the guitar solo on "Beat It," the audience nearly went through the floor! I even got goose bumps from the electric show of star power before me that hot and memorable night in Texas.

The next day the front page of the *Dallas Morning News* victoriously announced in its headline, "Michael Jackson Conquers," while a completely glowing review was titled, "After the Hype, Jacksons Come Through." Even the doubting *Dallas Times Herald* conceded in its page-one headline, "Startin' Somethin'—Fans Forget Controversy As Michael Sings." From that point on, it became clear that after conquering hard-to-please Dallas, the Victory tour was on the right track and it was full steam ahead!

Josh and I left Kansas City on Tuesday, July 10—and if I thought it was warm there, the 104-degree weather in Dallas really showed me what summer heat waves are all about! I thought I was going to melt like a candle a couple of times that week.

From the minute he stepped into town, Michael Jackson was all over the newspapers. It was common knowledge that Michael and his family were staying in the chic and ultramodern Anatole's hotel. The Jackson party occupied the whole nineteenth floor, and in order to get the computerized elevator to even stop there, a special code had to be entered on the control panel. Fans camped out in the lobby day and night in hopes of a single glimpse of the famed superstar—or at least one of the Jackson brothers. In one of the hotel's restaurants, I saw Jackson fans stop

Michael's father, Joseph Jackson, for autographs after his lunch.

Clever Michael spent much of his time in town in various disguises as he managed to sneak out of the hotel incognito. Jackson sightings had become as avidly rumored and followed as reports of UFOs from other planets. One afternoon at the shopping mall the Galleria, Michael was discovered disguised as an old man, with a gray wig and an overcoat pulled up around him. His shopping spree was interrupted twenty minutes into it as news of his presence spread from Marshall Field to Saks Fifth Avenue. After that he had to be whisked out of the mall by his bodyguards.

On Tuesday evening at about 7:30, Michael—who was dressed in a green shirt, blue jeans, and a floppy hat—his mother, and two burly bodyguards slipped out of the hotel lobby into a brown Chevrolet van and drove into a nearby town known as Carrollton. Pulling up to a house on Lakewood Drive, Michael and Katherine Jackson were ushered into the home of Wallace Lozano by a bodyguard. In the house Michael met other members of the Jehovah's Witnesses Church at a weekly Bible study meeting. After about an hour, lights on the porch were flashed once as a signal and the bodyguards came to the house to retrieve Jackson and his mother and take them back to the van. The next day Michael reportedly went from door to door with members of the Farmers Branch Jehovah's Witnesses congregation to talk to people about their religious beliefs.

After Michael made the announcement that he was going to donate all his earnings from the tour to charity, charitable contributions became a key concern at each stop along the tour. The Jacksons donated 1,200 tickets to underprivileged children, while the Pepsi-Cola Corporation donated an additional 1,300 tickets, valued at $39,000.

At high noon in the middle of Bell Plaza in downtown Dallas, it was 98 degrees in the shade. It was there that Pepsi-Cola presented eleven-year-old Ladonna Jones with her set of four tickets, and she drew additional winners for free tickets to the Texas Stadium concerts. When I got to

Bell Plaza at 11:00 A.M., the crowd was already gathering. While I waited for the presentation to start, I spoke to Helene Denney, the director of the Multiple Sclerosis Society, who was there to pick up the tickets donated to her organization. I was curious about the ticket distribution as well as the skepticism that seemed to hang over Dallas the day before the Jacksons' Dallas Victory debut.

Explained Helene, "We will select certain patients because there are certain patients who cannot go out into the heat, so we won't even tempt them with the tickets because the heat does destroy multiple sclerosis [victims]—they can't function. We will select patients, and that's a tough one to do. We will probably pick multiple sclerosis patients who have childen, who are not very well endowed with money, and could not even think about affording tickets."

"So in some cases, it will be children of the patients?" I asked.

"Yes," she continued. "I know one particular instance: she has teenaged children and she's restricted to the bed, so this would be of benefit to her, because we not only treat the patient, we treat the family too. So we will use it for selected patients, and I believe we will also use it for selected board members or volunteers who have worked for the Multiple Sclerosis Society."

I then asked, "How do you feel about Michael Jackson donating all of his proceeds from the concert tour to charity? Is this something you've seen other celebrities do, or is this completely unique?"

"Not too many celebrities, unless I just don't know about it. It's really quite nice—very nice, in fact! It's very worthwhile," she answered.

And then I asked the important query: "There was a lot of bad publicity about the original ticketing policy here in Dallas. Do you think Michael has turned the tide of public opinion by donating all his money to charity?"

Helene concluded, "I think so, because he probably couldn't have picked a better way of doing it than giving it to charity, because the community is so charity minded.

Dallas is a rather odd town. It takes a lot for them to forgive. An example is when the Cowboys [football team] went on strike. This community didn't forgive them very easily. I've found it unique to Dallas that they don't forgive very easily. I think that by Michael making such a *generous* change and offer, I think that will have a great deal to do with it."

Right after I spoke with Helene, a limousine pulled up in Bell Plaza and out popped Ladonna Jones, the shy sixth grader who had written the letter to Michael that had changed the lottery ticketing policy for the rest of the tour. Wearing a red and white striped Pepsi T-shirt and a new pair of blue jeans and new red shoes from a Pepsi-sponsored shopping spree, Ladonna was accompanied by her aunt Annette Russell.

If you think Michael Jackson is shy, you should have tried talking to Ladonna that hot day. A very cute little girl, it was obvious to me that she had no idea whatsoever the effect that her letter had on the media, Michael, and the tour itself. My brief conversation with her went as follows:

MARK: How does it feel to have changed the whole ticketing policy of the Jacksons' concerts for other kids? [No reply.] Do you feel proud that you've changed things?

LADONNA: Yes.

MARK: Are you still a big Michael Jackson fan?

LADONNA: Yeah.

MARK: Are you excited about the concert?

LADONNA: Yes.

MARK: Are you finding all of this attention to be fun?

LADONNA: Kind of.

MARK: Were you surprised to have heard from Michael?

LADONNA: Yeah.

MARK: Did you think your letter would get to him?

LADONNA: No.

*   *   *

Following that, Ladonna and a Michael Jackson look-alike named Fred Henry drew the names of twenty additional ticket winners, and a few city officials and Pepsi representatives spoke about the significance of the concerts and the charitable donations. While the sounds of the *Victory* album played, the crowd dispersed.

Directly after the press conference, Ken Ross, Josh, and I retrieved my car, which was parked on—I swear it's true—Jackson Street. We drove off to have frozen margaritas and Mexican food at a local Tex-Mex restaurant. Speaking of Mexican food, that is what Michael Jackson himself was eating in Texas. Press reports confirmed that a personal Sikh chef was touring with him. The chef, Mani Khalsa, was the owner of the Los Angeles vegetarian restaurant the Golden Temple. A strict vegetarian, Michael's favorite dish on the tour was New Mexican enchiladas made with meatless red chili sauce in tortillas of stone-ground wheat flour and topped off with melted low-sodium cheese.

The web of security at Texas Stadium that week was very intense. In fact, it was three times what was usually employed for any Dallas Cowboys game. The hand-held metal detectors were in full use, with 340 security officers on duty.

Pepsi set up two huge inflatable twenty-five-foot-high cans of Pepsi-Cola outside the stadium as an advertisement for their famous soft drink. The parking lot opened late Friday afternoon at 5:00, but the doors to the stadium didn't open until 6:30, so many people huddled under the shade of the giant Pepsi cans to escape the scorching heat, which was a solid 100 degrees late in the afternoon. It was also in the shadows of those huge Pepsi cans that the ever-sleazy ticket-scalping scene was going on. People walked around with pieces of cardboard bearing messages like "Need 2 tickets!" scrawled across them. A lot of scalpers on opening night in Dallas got stung by trying to sell the tickets for up to $100 each, but as the show started, they were letting them go for as little as $5. On the subsequent nights, rumors of $5 tickets brought a lot of people to the stadium in hopes of a real bargain, but the joke was on them when they discovered that the scalpers wouldn't part with their tickets for less than $75 each. It was a supply-and-demand game that was repeated in city after city, with many disappointed people left without the bargain tickets they thought they'd find on second and third nights.

Before the show Friday night, Ladonna Jones was taken backstage to meet her idol. Once in the inner sanctum she was mesmerized at finally meeting Michael Jackson in person. They chatted for a moment, and he gave her a kiss on the cheek and signed a copy of the Jacksons' *Victory* album with the inscription, "Love, Michael Jackson 1984 XXX." For her, the last week and a half had been a Michael Jackson fan's dream come true!

Texas Stadium is actually located in Irving, Texas, between downtown and the Dallas airport. The architectural design of the roof absolutely takes the cake for stupidity! When they were constructing it, they ran out of money in the middle of the project, and instead of just making it an open-air stadium, they built a partial roof that makes the stadium very uncomfortable. Since there is a huge hole the size of a football field in the center of the partial roof, it cannot be air-conditioned, and because of its shape it is impossible for the air to circulate, and if it rains you still get wet. Friday night, even though the sun had gone down, inside the stadium it was still 100 degrees, muggy, and without a breath of moving air. That weekend approximately one hundred people were treated for heat-related illnesses inside Texas Stadium.

However, matching the heat of the air on opening night in Dallas was an excitingly hot audience. It was Friday the thirteenth, and an eerie full moon hung in the Texas sky overhead. Before the show even started, the audience was going berserk as David Lee Roth of Van Halen's group paraded through the crowd. People screamed ecstatically as Prince marched in and found a seat. In addition, tiny Emmanuel Lewis of the TV show *Webster* was seated in a chair in the fenced-in bottom part of the lighting tower.

As the house lights went down at 9:30 P.M., the audience was totally out of control and screaming with glee. From the very beginning of the concert, it was clear that this was going to be one of the best nights on the whole tour. Michael was obviously rested, refreshed, and into the excitement of his fans.

In the middle of the show, right before he went into "Human Nature," Michael looked down at the people dancing on their chairs in the floor seats, carrying on, and having a great time. Noticing that the security guards were trying to get the people to sit back down, Michael interjected into the microphone, "Hey, security people! You've got to let these kids stand up in front!" And then to the kids he announced, "Do anything you want to do.... You having fun?" They screamed back in unison, "Yeah!" and it was on with the show.

The huge screen above the stage on which the close-up images were projected was much better and clearer in resolution than the Diamond Vision screen at Arrowhead, and other obvious improvements had taken place since the previous weekend in Kansas City. The mock argument between the brothers which preceded Jermaine's solo spot in Kansas City was totally cut out for the rest of the tour, and the group went directly into "Let's Get Serious." After that song, Jermaine announced, "We're gonna dedicate this to our brother Jackie who is not with us," referring to his ballad "Do You Like Me."

By this point in the show, I was absolutely dripping wet with perspiration from the heat, but the enthusiasm from the crowd helped me ignore the temperature. It was already the most exciting show on the tour yet. When it came time for the Jacksons to do "Beat It," all of us in the audience were cheering like crazy. In the middle of the song, when Michael announced "Eddie Van Halen!" and the nimble-fingered guitarist suddenly appeared in a bright spotlight from stage right and dove into the searing guitar solo that he made famous on the record, we all went wild. The screams alone nearly blew the silly half roof off the stadium. The crowd snapped, clapped, screamed, and hollered as Michael danced to Eddie's sizzling sounds.

After the closing fireworks at the end of the concert, a tape of "State Of Shock" was played as well as several cuts from the *Victory* album while the exhausted crowd dispersed. That first night in Dallas still sticks out in my mind as one of the best nights of the whole tour!

Again, the audiences in Dallas were as orderly as they had been in Kansas City. The only real hassle on opening night in Texas was a phony bomb threat. At 9:50 P.M. first-aid personnel were called to immediately man their stations while security guards searched for the nonexistent bomb, but it turned out to be nothing more than a crank call. According to Chuck Sullivan, "We had our security people go through all of the washrooms and check all the waste-baskets." But he concluded, "It was a crank thing."

Saturday and Sunday nights in Dallas (July 14 and 15) saw a further evolution of the show. Jermaine's ballad "Do You Like Me" was cut altogether without a replacement (until Newark, New Jersey), and from that point on "Let's Get Serious" was introduced with the question, "Do you want to get serious?" which was shouted out from the stage during the blackout light cue that followed Michael's "She's Out Of My Life."

On Sunday night in Dallas, the temperature in Texas Stadium hit 104 degrees. From that evening on, Randy's conga solo during "Working Day And Night" was expanded and highlighted even further. Also, that night some of the stars from the TV series *Dallas* showed up in the audience. Seated in private boxes were cast members Larry Hagman, Linda Gray, Charlene Tilton, and Patrick Duffy.

That sweltering weekend in July, Michael Jackson and his musical brothers scored the most decisive victory that Texas had seen since the Battle of the Alamo! The next stop on their whirlwind tour was the Florida city that bears Michael's family name: Jacksonville.

JACKSONVILLE, FLORIDA

According to a report in the popular nationally distributed daily newspaper *USA Today*, the city of Jacksonville had to make many concessions to make it possible for the Jacksons to appear at the Gator Bowl on July 21, 22, and 23. This was the third series of three weekend concerts, completing the initial leg of the Victory tour, and the controversies were still raging. The July 2, cover story in *USA Today* said that:

> Jacksons' tour promoter Charles Sullivan will pay Jacksonville Fla. $75,000 for the use of the Gator Bowl for three concerts July 21–23. In return Sullivan gets:
>
> Up to $6.3 million from the sale of 210,000 tickets.
>
> Interest from lottery ticket orders held 4–6 weeks.
>
> Estimated $40,000 from food, drink concessions.
>
> 77.5 percent of souvenir revenue and 28 percent of rental revenue from cushions, binoculars.
>
> Up to $120,000 from parking (half going to charity).
>
> Technical services and equipment—stagehands, utilities, generators, ushers—worth up to $320,000 being paid by city.
>
> $125,000 in promotion and advertising paid by city. Source: City of Jacksonville, Fla.

Although Michael had abolished the lottery ticket sales two weeks before, when I arrived in Jacksonville the controversies still raged on. The issue in many highly publicized verbal and print-media debates was, should the city have agreed to spend $445,000 to lure the Jacksons' Victory tour to Jacksonville in the interest of increased tourist dollars?

Again, as in Kansas City and Dallas, once Michael Jackson rolled into town, all the problems seemed to vanish with the initial notes of his magical singing.

That week in July there were three major national news stories: (1) the Democratic National Convention, (2) the Miss America scandal, and (3) the Victory tour. The respective outcome of these issues resulted in America's first female Vice Presidential candidate, the first Miss America to ever be forced to resign, and another decisive victory for Michael!

On Friday night, July 20, I received a phone call from Jay Moore from radio station WIVY, whom I had met that morning. According to Jay, two friends of his who own bookstores in the San Marco area of Jacksonville, stores which specialize in rare and out-of-print books and magazines, had each had a very interesting visitor—a young black man with an obviously false mustache, a baggy gray suit, dark glasses, and a dark hat pulled down over his eyes. The mysterious young man was accompanied by two burly football linebacker-sized bodyguards, and in a soft voice asked to be shown where the children's and religious books were located. Need I say more? It was naturally none other than Michael Jackson himself, out on another one of his famous incognito shopping sprees.

On Saturday afternoon Jay took me over to meet both store owners. According to Mike Blauer of the San Marco Book Store, he had his suspicions about the identity of his oddly dressed customer, which were confirmed after he spoke to him. Said Blauer, "After about ten minutes of us just wondering out loud, I walked up to his two assistants, just like I do to other customers, and I just said, 'Are there any particular books I can help you find?' and I turned the corner and Jackson was standing looking at my various books on plays. I said, 'Can I help you with any books?' He said [Blauer used a high pitched voice], 'Oh, no thank you, I'm just looking.'" After Blauer heard the familiar voice, he knew for sure that it was the real Michael Jackson.

According to Blauer, the bodyguards stuck very close to

Jackson the entire time he was in the store. Michael spent part of his time sitting cross-legged on the floor, browsing through a couple of art books. Michael and his bodyguards then went next door to an interior decorating store, and it seems that Michael was most amused by a framed, autographed picture of his friend Brooke Shields that hung in the shop.

After the visit to the bookstore, Mike Blauer located a first-edition copy of the play *Peter Pan* and sent it over to the hotel where the Jackson crew was staying, with a note which said, "Is this what you were looking for?" Blauer never heard back from Jackson and was left with nothing more than an amusing story to tell his customers.

A couple of different and unique procedures were employed at the Jacksons' concerts in Jacksonville that Saturday, Sunday, and Monday. First of all, it was the first time that nonreserved "festival" seating would be sold for patrons on the field, or ground level, in front of the stage. Originally it was going to be a first come, first served, find-your-own-space type of situation, but it was later announced that five thousand seats would be set up on the field to avoid the possibility of people trampling each other for a ringside spot.

Also, since the mail-in ticket lottery had been abolished in the middle of the sales for the Jacksonville dates, Monday, July 23, saw the first time that Victory tickets were sold over the counter at a ticket booth. It was feared that there would be people fighting to get into line for the tickets, but the buyers were all very orderly and there were no problems.

One of my favorite souvenirs from the tour was a T-shirt that I bought at a nearby shopping mall that read "Michaelized In Jacksonville!" Très clever!

Speaking of souvenirs, on the first night of the Jacksonville dates, official "Jacksons Victory Tour" programs were on sale for $8 apiece. I knew that I had to have one for my collection, but I decided to wait until after the show. However, they had completely sold out all the programs that night. When I came back the next night, there was a fresh batch of programs, but—are you ready for this?—they were so successful that on Sunday night the price had become $10! Unbelievable! The program features thirty-two pages of full-color pinups of all six Jackson brothers, plus a list of the tour personnel. The photography of the Jacksons is beautiful, and the cover shot depicts the six brothers atop a jeep in pith helmets and safari outfits. They look like they're stalking wild animals through the jungle—like a herd of out-of-control Kreetons maybe? The official souvenir stands that weekend also saw the introduction of tiny silver rhinestone-studded white glove pins ($13) and the same tiny rhinestone-studded glove as a charm on a chain ($15).

Saturday, July 21, was the first of the three nights of Victory concerts at the Gator Bowl, and at 45,324 tickets sold, it was a certified sellout. That night as I took my seat, the sky was overcast with a 60 percent chance of rain. At the Gator Bowl there is an ordinance against bringing umbrellas to the stadium, so I dressed to get soaked. The temperatures that day were in the 80-degree range, and there was a nice light breeze in the stadium, so it was a vast improvement over the 100-degree temperatures of Dallas.

During the entire Victory tour, the opening act was rock and roll juggler Chris Bliss, who tossed brightly colored tennis-sized balls into the air in time to a number of jazz and rock songs. Many times the audiences ignored him, but usually when he got to the point where he juggled to the Beatles song "A Day In The Life" from the *Sgt. Pepper's Lonely Hearts Club Band* album, he caught the impatient crowd's attention. Chris knew that it was going to be difficult holding the audience's attention, realizing that they couldn't care less about seeing anybody on that stage but Michael and his brothers. After receiving a healthy round of applause at the close of his set that first night in Jacksonville, Chris joked from the stage, "Thank you for treating me like a performer and not like a human sacrifice!"

Before the show began that night, Michael met eight

children backstage who suffered from incurable diseases. One of the eight young fans was fourteen-year-old Malanda Cooper, who was suffering from sickle-cell anemia and might not live long enough to hear Michael's next solo album. She wrote a letter to Jacksonville Mayor Jake Godbold, saying that her one wish was to meet her idol. Godbold in turn sent a plea to Jackson. With everything else on his mind that night, Michael made the time to meet with terminally ill Malanda. Also in the audience that evening were seven hundred of Michael's "special guests," disadvantaged and/or handicapped kids who were treated to the best thriller night of their lives.

By 9:39 P.M. people were stomping their feet on the aluminum bleachers of the Gator Bowl like a herd of elephants, chanting in time, "Michael! Michael! Michael!" At 9:44 P.M. the lights went down to immediate screams, more stomping, and people holding up lit matches and cigarette lighters in the darkness to show their enthusiasm.

As always, the crowd went crazy as the Jacksons made their entrance onto the floor of the stage. While the show progressed, the skies overhead cleared up, making for a perfect night for the concert. Michael was in fine form, and when he went up on his toes during "Working Day And Night," a close-up of his feet on the huge projection screen drew shrieks of elation from his fans. From this night on, the drum solo at the end of "Beat It" was extended a bit longer, and the musicians jammed more on "Shake Your Body (Down To The Ground)."

One of the wildest new things that I noticed that night was a copper, gold, and black metallic jacket that Marlon wore that had flickering colored lights woven into it. He wore it a number of times during the tour, and when the stage went to blackouts, you could still see Marlon's battery-powered jacket twinkling away in the darkness.

On Sunday, July 22, it began raining at 1:15 in the afternoon, but it stopped about an hour later. It began raining again at 5:45 P.M., but had stopped by 7:20, and the skies cleared in time for the show. Before the show started that night, DJ Tom Joyner came out on stage and had the people chanting, "No rain! No rain! No rain!" Apparently it worked.

Just before the show, Michael's mother, Katherine Jackson, was ushered to seats set up in the bottom of the lighting tower in the middle of the field.

That night I sat in the press seats set up on the floor, and from the beginning of the Kreetons intro straight through to the fireworks extravaganza at the end, the people with field seats all stood and danced on top of their chairs. The crowd was so excited that they refused to sit down, so what else could I do but dance in my seat too!

On Monday, July 23, it was a beautiful day for an outdoor concert. In the clear skies over the Gator Bowl, a skywriting airplane circled overhead, spelling out the word "Pepsi" in the stratosphere, while another plane dragged a long banner behind it which read "A.T.&T. Long Distance, You Can't 'Beat It!'" Everyone wanted to get into the act!

That night a 3-D photographer was present to take pictures for special "Victory" reels for View-Master. They had also done a 3-D "Thriller" package which Michael liked so much that he invited them to shoot the concert.

In the audience that same evening were Lionel Richie and Patti LaBelle. Also present was the oldest Michael Jackson fan to attend the Victory concerts: 111-year-old Elija Mimms.

On Monday night Tito wore a white sequined baseball uniform on stage, trimmed in red and blue sequins, with his name on the front and "Jacksons" and the numeral "1" in glittering letters on the back. To complete the look, Tito's guitar was also in the baseball motif, with a bat for the handle and a huge brown-leather-covered baseball glove at the bottom. In the glove there was naturally a white baseball. Go for it, Tito!

The audiences the three nights in Florida were very enthusiastic, and the final outcome of the Jacksonville dates was highly profitable for the community and for the Jacksons as well. Mayor Jake Godbold's gamble in making the necessary concessions had paid off for his city. In fact, in drawing crowds of over 135,000 in three sold-out nights, Michael and his four brothers broke attendance records for Gator Bowl rock events, surpassing previous totals set by the Rolling Stones in 1975 (75,000), the Beatles in 1964 (20,000) and the Who in 1976 (15,000).

I noticed many improvements in the Jacksonville shows. The performance was even slicker and more supertight by this point in the tour. Michael looked as if he was having as much fun on stage as his fans were having watching him! All the light and sound cues were happening with split-second timing, and it was the perfect time to take the show north to meet the often hard to please New York critics.

NEW JERSEY, NEW YORK, AND KNOXVILLE

When I had arrived in Kansas City, Missouri, on July 6, the press people were given detailed itineraries for the thirteen cities the Victory tour would be playing, with the finale in Anaheim, California—appropriately the home of Michael's famous home away from home, Disneyland (November 7 and 8). This solidified schedule gave all us journalists, and the world in general, a feeling (or illusion) that after all the confusion, mixed signals, and false starts, the tour was indeed on course, well planned, and totally under control. Well, guess what? We were all wrong—the mass confusion was just beginning.

Rumors of changes began right after the first three concerts played Kansas City, with complete confusion reigning for the entire duration of the tour. In most instances, Michael Jackson fans were kept dangling on a string, with tickets going on sale mere days before the actual concerts took place. In spite of Michael's indisputable and incredible charisma on stage, the tour planning was still a total, embarrassing mess!

The "new official" schedule was not even a week old

and it was already out of date. The first rumor was that
Washington, D.C., had been added to the itinerary for July
28 and 29. It was on. It was off. It was on again, and then
it was officially off. Next the four dates at Madison Square
Garden in New York City were in danger of being canceled
in favor of the Meadowlands Sports Complex in East
Rutherford, New Jersey, across the Hudson River from
Manhattan. It was evident that no one knew for sure what
was going to happen after Jacksonville when the Jacksons
opened there on July 21. I was already driving my travel
agent crazy. Finally, on Sunday, July 22, it was announced
that two Madison Square Garden dates were off, three
Meadowlands dates were added, and Washington, D.C.,
would probably host Victory in late September.

Would Michael's fans jump like Pavlov's dogs when they
heard that tickets in their area were suddenly on sale? Is the
Pope Catholic? Well, the answer to both of these questions
is of course yes, and on that Sunday morning when the New
York area dates were announced, in a period of less than
nine hours, all 167,000 Victory tickets had been sold for
both the Meadowlands (July 29, 30, and 31) and Madison
Square Garden (August 4 and 5).

According to the tour promoter and head of Stadium
Management Corporation, Chuck Sullivan, the Victory show
stood to lose money to the tune of $100,000 per night for
both nights it played Madison Square Garden because only
16,000 of the Garden's 18,000 capacity could be utilized,
whereas at the Meadowlands, which has an 80,000-seat
capacity, 45,000 tickets could be sold with total visibility.
Michael and his brothers were quite insistent that the
Madison Square Garden dates—at least two of them, be
kept. After all, how can you have the megatour of the
century and not play in the media capital of the world? Said
Marlon Jackson on the subject, "The Garden shows will be
better than the outdoor show. The audience is a lot closer
to you, and you get a vibe between you and the audience
you can relate to."

To further complicate things, Indianapolis, Indiana, had

its dates canceled toward the end of July, and it looked as if Champaign, Illinois, was going to pick up the August 17 and 18 time slots, but by July 30 that idea had also been dropped. On July 29 Chuck Sullivan announced that if he could convince the Jacksons, the tour would be extended on into December, with a grand finale on Christmas Day in Aloha Stadium in Hawaii. However, this plan was shot down by mid-August at a press briefing in Detroit. Complete uncertainty and conflicting reports continued to prevail as the Victory tour rolled on into the vast unknown.

But, enough about the baffling illogic of the tour "planning"... and on with the show!

THE MEADOWLANDS

When I arrived at LaGuardia Airport on Sunday, July 29, in time for that evening's first New Jersey concert, I picked up a copy of the *New York Times* to find an article titled "Variety of Scalpers Peddling Jackson Seats for Up to $700!" Yes, I'm dead serious—$700! For both the Meadowlands and Madison Square Garden concerts, scalpers' tickets were generally in the vicinity of $125 to $200 each, but the tour's record was indeed a classified ad placed by a man living in Delaware who offered a "front-row center" seat for sale at the astronomical sum of $700. It was then that I realized I was indeed in for a rare treat for these five New Jersey and New York Jackson shows. When New Yorkers really get into something, you know it's going to be a real media extravaganza!

Opening night of the three Meadowlands concerts was kicked off with a fantastic press reception held at the Stadium Club on the premises of the concert, and hosted by the Jacksons, Epic Records, and Stadium Management Corporation. All of my rock and roll journalist friends were on hand, as it seemed every major magazine, newspaper, and television station was also. I was especially impressed to find that the *New York Post* had sent its Broadway reviewer,

Clive Barnes, to critique the show—and he loved it!

In the audience that warm Sunday night at Giants Stadium in the Meadowlands Sports Complex were Michael's mother, his sister Janet Jackson, actor Erik Estrada, Yoko Ono and her son Sean Lennon, and video director Bob Giraldi. After Chris Bliss's juggling act, older brother Jackie Jackson hobbled out onto the stage on his crutches and waved to the audience. That was the first time he was seen on the Victory tour. The crowd was so psyched up for the show, they even cheered the fog machines when they were being tested before the show. The audience was completely into the event being a total "happening." Every New York-area music critic within a fifty-mile radius was there that night in East Rutherford, New Jersey, and the Jacksons delivered one of their most truly sharp and inspired shows. Although this was the tenth consecutive time that I had seen the show, I literally got goose bumps from the uncontrollably enthusiastic audience response to the group's rising out of the floor of the stage. Michael was especially up for the energy-charged night.

Beating out the rhythm of "Off The Wall" on a cow bell, Tito helped whip the crowd into a frenzy while his younger brother Michael mesmerized and stunned his throngs of adoring worshippers. The gloved one really gave us his all that evening!

That same Sunday night saw a great new addition to the show—in fact, the first one that the tour had seen. Despite rumors that something would be added from the *Victory* album, that turned out not to be the addition. Right after he finished singing "Let's Get Serious," Jermaine announced, "I'd like to do a song from my new album, *Dynamite*." It was an excellent choice to replace "Do You Like Me," which had been dropped in Dallas. The song "Dynamite" was listed as one of the "most added" radio singles the previous week in *Billboard* magazine, and looked as if it would be an explosive hit for him. It was a tasty addition to the group's virtual buffet menu of hits served up in the Victory show!

The crowd response during that evening's concert was the strongest yet; the show was gaining slickness with every performance.

The next night Jermaine in particular looked as if he was having a good time. He was much more relaxed about the way things were going on stage. Everyone loved "Dynamite," and at long last Jermaine looked confident that the middle song of his three lead-singing turns was strong.

Before the show on Monday, the crowd got into something that I had never witnessed before. To entertain themselves before the show started, people were sequentially standing, raising their arms, cheering, and sitting back down in their seats. The visual effect was as if rippling waves of clockwise electric activity had hit them. The motion, which began with a handful of people, soon spread to the whole sold-out crowd of 45,000. When the show got going, they proved to be even more into the event, and continued to cheer with the same kinetic flair.

On Tuesday, July 31, the third Victory night at the Meadowlands saw an added surprise guest as Jackie Jackson hobbled out onto the stage on his crutches during "I'll Be There" and sang harmony vocals with his brothers. It was the first time during the summer that he made an on-stage appearance singing with his five younger brothers, so it was quite a special highlight! All three of the shows at the Meadowlands went successfully. Now, preceded by glowing reviews and with much pomp and circumstance, it was time to play the smallest and most prestigious venue of their tour: Manhattan's famous show business institution, the indoor arena Madison Square Garden, in the heart of New York City!

MADISON SQUARE GARDEN

At the Sunday night "press debriefing" at the Meadowlands, Chuck Sullivan informed us eager media scribes that the two dates at Madison Square Garden would be significant for many reasons. Not only was it the smallest arena that the Victory tour would play, but it would also be the most heavily guarded as well. Not only would the massive stage scaffolding be absent from the arena, but weighing in at 60,000 pounds, all the Jacksons' sound and lighting equipment would be hanging suspended from the ceiling, making this the heaviest load ever to be held from overhead in the history of Madison Square Garden!

Crime, riots, and outrageously volatile security risks— all of these concerns hung like a potential black cloud over the Jacksons' two performances at New York City's famed Garden.

When I was doing one of my weekly Australian Victory tour radio broadcasts, I explained to the show's producer, Vesna Mezic, that the Jacksons were going to play at Madison Square Garden. To which she replied over the telephone from Adelaide, Australia, "Isn't that a lovely setting—Michael Jackson singing in the middle of a lot of flowers in a garden!" I had to explain to her, "No, no, no, Vesna, it's not a lovely flower-filled garden, it's a huge concrete arena in the middle of Manhattan!"

Two specific events stuck out in everybody's mind when it was announced that the Jacksons would be performing at Madison Square Garden. In 1981, when the group last played there, uncontrollable juvenile delinquents went on a criminal rampage of chain snatching and mugging during the concert. And only one year before, in July 1983, at a free Diana Ross concert in the middle of Central Park, hordes of hoodlums trampled, beat up, and mugged people in the audience, causing the city to ban all rock concerts in the park to protect citizens' safety. That brings us to the Victory concerts at the Garden, where heavy-metal groups like Black Sabbath have attracted the most undesirable bands of troublemakers imaginable.

New York City Mayor Ed Koch, the Jacksons, and the City of New York were not under any circumstances going to let another fiasco like these mar the Victory tour. According to Chuck Sullivan at his Meadowlands press brief-

(Copyright © 1984 Ebet Roberts)

Twelve-year-old Ladonna Jones wrote the letter that changed the Victory ticketing policy. Here she picks additional ticket winners in Dallas, Texas. *(Joshua Touster)*

(Joshua Touster)

(Joshua Touster)

JERMAINE JACKSON *(Copyright © 1984 Ebet Roberts)*

"His Hotness" *(Copyright © 1984 Ebet Roberts)*

... his fans!
(Joshua Touster)

(Joshua Touster)

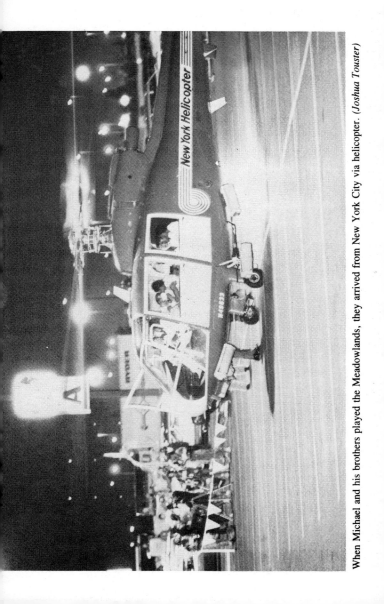

When Michael and his brothers played the Meadowlands, they arrived from New York City via helicopter. *(Joshua Touster)*

Randy, Jermaine, & Marlon "get serious"! *(Copyright © 1984 Ebet Roberts)*

A group of Michael Jackson fans stage their own version of Thriller while they wait for the show to begin at the Meadowlands in New Jersey. *(Joshua Touster)*

Fireworks crown the Meadowlands at the sizzling Jacksons finale. *(Joshua Touster)*

(Joshua Touster)

(Joshua Touster)

When Michael came to Manhattan, even New York City's Mayor Ed Koch put on his one white glove and got into the act! *(N.Y. Daily News Photo)*

Yoko Ono arrives to see Michael's Victory *(Copyright © 1984 Ebet Roberts)*

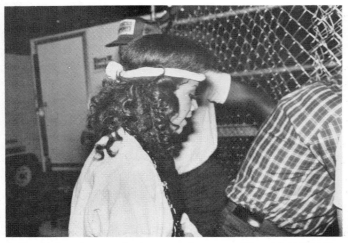

LaToya Jackson is escorted to her seat at the concert. *(Copyright © 1984 Ebet Roberts)*

(Copyright © 1984 Ebet Roberts)

Although all sorts of controversy raged over the $30 ticket prices to the Victory show, in each city the Jacksons played every limousine in town seemed to be rented out by Michael's fans! *(Joshua Touster)*

(Joshua Touster)

(Joshua Touster)

(Joshua Touster)

(Joshua Touster)

(Joshua Touster)

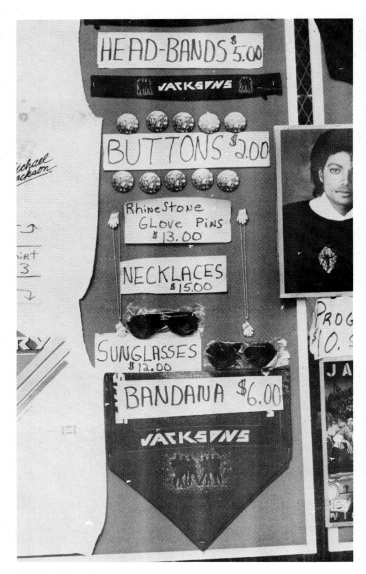

(Joshua Touster)

(*Joshua Touster*)

(*Joshua Touster*)

(Copyright © 1984 Ebet Roberts)

Victory tour promoter, Chuck Sullivan. *(Joshua Touster)*

Dethroned promoter Don King. *(Joshua Touster)*

(Joshua Touster)

(Joshua Touster)

(Joshua Touster)

(Joshua Touster)

(Joshua Touster)

(Joshua Touster)

(Joshua Touster)

(Joshua Touster)

(Joshua Touster)

ing, "there will be very substantial security" measures taken. Sullivan went on, "These shows not only will be the most heavily secured on the tour, but the most heavily secured event in the history of the Garden. We've had twelve straight victories in terms of not having any incidents, and we're going for two more this weekend."

To accomplish this goal, more than two thousand uniformed, plainclothes, and mounted New York City police officers were on duty that evening. According to the police department's chief of operations, Robert Johnson, "We never had a plan like this, but we never had a personality like Michael Jackson." From Fifth Avenue west, and from Twenty-Third Street north, I personally witnessed four police officers on every single street corner around Madison Square Garden. The area between Seventh and Eighth avenues, and between Thirty-third and Thirty-first streets was established as the "frozen zone," which was a four-block area in which an individually held ticket had to be shown to gain entry. There was only one way into Madison Square Garden those two nights, and that was through a barrier-lined passageway on Thirty-first street. Patrons had to enter either on Seventh or Eighth avenues, and had to pass by rows of policemen and policewomen, up a winding trail toward the Garden's eastern entrance. There was at least one armed police officer every ten feet—and that was in the sparsest areas of protection. As paranoid as I am when it comes to potentially dangerous situations, I can honestly attest that I have never felt more safe in my entire decade of living in the heart of New York City!

On the canopy over the entrance to the New York Penta Hotel (formerly the Statler Hilton) stood six forty-foot-tall busts of the Jackson brothers and a banner which read "Pepsi Presents The Jacksons." That's the same hotel that Glenn Miller's 1940s hit song "PEnnsylvania 6-5000" was written about. That weekend the hotel looked conspicuously as if it belonged to another generation's musical dynasty—that of the Jacksons!

During his juggling act, Chris Bliss said to the well-ordered audience, "You're very lucky — you get to see the 'living-room show'!" Indeed, it was just that — intimate, comfortable, and well-mannered. I never in my wildest dreams thought that I'd ever feel that way in the middle of 16,000 people in Madison Square Garden, but the experience *was* intimate in comparison to the rest of the Victory tour. Not only were the stage's massive scaffolding base and the scrims of the huge trees missing, but gone was the giant video projection screen as well.

Heading the "Life" section in the Wednesday, August 1, 1984, edition of *USA Today* was a bold item in the regular feature "Today's Tip-Off," which read "Mick will join Michael . . . and the rest of The Jacksons on stage Saturday at New York's Madison Square Garden. Jagger and Mr. Thriller will perform their hit 'State Of Shock,' No. 3 on the charts this week, off The Jacksons' 'Victory' LP." Chuck Sullivan confirmed the rumor in that Friday's edition. Unfortunately, it never did happen. I had heard the persistent rumor that Jagger was due to show up at one of the concerts to tape a video of the historic duet live on stage — but it was not to materialize during either of these nights in New York, which was a big disappointment. However, what I did witness in the Garden was two excellent evenings of Michael, Randy, Marlon, Jermaine, and Tito. And on Sunday night I could see Jackie harmonizing along with his brothers from a point lower than the stage, in the wing space off to stage right.

During the Saturday performance, as "Off The Wall" began, Michael yelled out to the audience, "Don't sit down — I want you to dance and have a good time!" And believe me, we did just that! Saturday night I spotted Andy Warhol in the crowd, and on Sunday night Mayor Koch, Cyndi Lauper, Pia Zadora, Bette Midler, John Denver, Neil Sedaka, Peter Frampton, Brooke Shields, and Emmanuel Lewis were present to cheer Michael on. One night in Manhattan, Michael had dinner with Katharine Hepburn at her New York town house.

After the show on Sunday night, I attended a party that

Arista Records gave for Jermaine at the Limelight disco. As the party's entertainment, the Shirelles sang, and Whitney Houston (Dionne Warwick's niece) demonstrated her vocal skills. The party closed with Whitney and Jermaine doing their duet "Take Good Care Of My Heart."

With all the potential danger that the Madison Square Garden dates posed, they went incredibly smoothly and were two of the highlights of the entire tour. The energy level of the Saturday crowd was a bit subdued, perhaps due to the "1984"-style police-state atmosphere, but the Sunday night crowd couldn't have cared less. They came to "party down," and that is exactly what they did, in an orderly, fun fashion.

And you thought *New York City* was such a dangerous town? Well, what followed in the next city almost finished off the entire Victory tour!

DEATH THREATS IN KNOXVILLE

On Monday, August 6, I flew home to Detroit for a family gathering, and that night on the eleven o'clock news came word that Michael Jackson's life had been threatened and that the upcoming weekend concerts at the University of Tennessee's Neyland Stadium had been postponed indefinitely! However, in the newspapers the next morning there were conflicting reports as to the fate of the Knoxville concerts. The originally planned August 10 and 11 tour dates had sold so well that a concert on Friday, August 9, had been added, but now all three were in danger of turning into a complete disaster. And what, the world asked, would happen to the rest of the tour? Already the Indianapolis and Champaign dates had fallen through, and contracts had yet to be signed for Detroit. Would death threats spell the demise of the Victory tour?

According to Knoxville DJ Bob Anderson, who is known to his listeners on WOKI-FM as "Bandit," complete chaos reigned in that city on Monday when news spread of threatening letters received by the *Knoxville News-Sentinel* and by the University of Tennessee. According to Anderson, the concerts were called off in the afternoon but were back on again late that night.

As Bob explained it to me, "We confirmed that it indeed had been postponed and continued to run announcements to that effect. Of course it was the big story on the local six o'clock news in this city, and all over the state, that the shows had been postponed. No further word was available other than that there were some threats made against the Jacksons, and that's all there was. So we were sitting there informing the entire state, and I'm sure most of the nation by that point knew about it, that the entire engagement had been indefinitely postponed. At a little after 11:00 P.M. we were informed that the shows were on again, which I'm sure caused pandemonium. The next day it was like, 'Oops— never mind!'"

Anderson continued, "There was no further explanation until Bob Sullivan [tour coordinator] held a press conference on Wednesday saying that they had carefully analyzed the letters and had held meetings with the Jacksons themselves, with their security people, and with the FBI, and felt that the concerts could be held without a problem to either the Jacksons or to the fans that were coming. But it sure turned this town upside down, and I'm sure most of the state totally upside down for a period from 3:00 P.M. to 11:30 P.M. It was a big enough story in Knoxville that the local newsman in this town interrupted the telecast of the Olympics to say that the Jacksons' tour was back on again!"

Both threats were printed word for word in the Wednesday edition of the *Knoxville News-Sentinel*, each in its own sick way predicting that Michael Jackson would be assassinated on stage and many of his fans would perish along with him. Each of the letters was obviously the work of a very disturbed individual who had nothing better to do with his time than cause problems.

The FBI was called in to analyze the threats, and according to their findings, the letters were simply unfounded threats that posed no serious danger to the safety of Michael or the audience. However, matters like these are not to be taken lightly, and many precautions had to be taken to insure the safety of everyone who attended the concert.

Said Chuck Sullivan of the situation, "If we can play metro New York for five dates without an incident, I know we can play three dates in Knoxville. We couldn't be [intimidated] by this sort of thing or we'd be getting threats all the way."

Security measures were tightened, and reportedly there were armed sharpshooters stationed on the rooftops of tall buildings on the university grounds which surround the stadium. Police cars with trained attack dogs in them were quite evident at the Friday night concert, as were riot-helmeted Knoxville policemen with pistols and nightsticks. From the day the threats were made public until the three concerts were over, no one was allowed in the stadium without being frisked from head to toe, including Chuck Sullivan and Michael's personal staff. No risks were to be taken. Entering the stadium that weekend also entailed an extra-thorough rundown with metal detectors. The hand-held detectors were set so sensitively that car keys and pockets full of change set them off and had to be visually examined before guards let anyone enter Neyland Stadium. One security guard told me that more than once she discovered concealed firearms on plainclothes police officers who were then detained while badges and credentials were checked.

Once inside Neyland Stadium, I found my seat and began talking to James McBride of *People* magazine, and the Jacksons' publicist, Howard Bloom. At 9:10 P.M., in the middle of our conversation, it began to rain. The tickets for that engagement had the message "Rain or Shine" clearly printed on them, so there was nothing to do but sit in the rain until it ended. By 9:46 the rain stopped, I put away my umbrella, and the stage was mopped dry for the show to begin. Between the rain and the death threats, not all the tickets had been sold for Friday night's show. At 48,783 tickets sold, it was the first Victory show that was not a sellout, and yet it was still the biggest crowd on the tour to that point!

At 9:57 the stadium lights went down and the show began. One glimpse of Michael Jackson and his brothers ascending toward the spotlights from the floor of the stage and all the problems that had plagued the Knoxville dates melted away. Nobody's spirits were dampened that night by either the rain or the death threats. Once the music started, it was business as usual.

Right before he went into "Human Nature," Michael announced to the crowd, "It's so wonderful to be here, I just want to say, I love you very much." It was his way of relieving the anxiety that had plagued the town, the tour, and the confused fans that tense week in Tennessee.

The fireworks after the show that night were the best yet on the tour. In fact, they were excellent all three nights in Knoxville. In the Meadowlands, they were subdued because the stadium was right in the flight pattern for Newark Airport (could you see them shooting down a Boeing 747 in the middle of the concert with a skyrocket?), and at indoor Madison Square Garden there was only so much that could be done pyrotechnically at the end of the show without blowing the roof off.

At the press debriefing after the show, Chuck Sullivan announced that "we feel this is the greatest victory of the Victory tour." With regard to the threats, he said, "Even with the letters, Michael Jackson felt that it was important enough for his fans to play this date."

For an added bit of security, each night Michael was transported to Neyland Stadium in an armored Wells Fargo truck. Upon arriving backstage at the stadium, he disappeared into his dressing room, which was full of velvet-upholstered Victorian furniture and draped in yellow and blue tapestries. Abounding were floral arrangements decorated with balloons and white sequined gloves. For security reasons, Michael's mother, Katherine Jackson, was asked to remain backstage for the duration of the show. Also, during his stay in Knoxville Michael was advised not to don any of his disguises and go out on incognito shopping sprees or do any religious canvassing as he had done in previous cities on the tour.

On Friday night in Knoxville, many scalpers were caught holding handfuls of tickets when the concert began. That night, in all the confusion they could not get rid of them at the last minute. A story in Saturday's *Knoxville News-Sentinel* pointed up the situation with the humorous headline "Scalpers Choke On 'Ticket Salad.'" Tickets sales were not a problem on Saturday or Sunday in Knoxville, which recorded record crowds at 50,239 (a sellout) and 49,485, respectively.

Sunday night's Knoxville crowd was the most enthusiastic of the three dates in that city. Michael was obviously relieved that nothing had gone wrong the nights before, and appeared very into the excitement of the performance that evening. In fact, on "Wanna Be Startin' Something," he executed one of his spins so fast that he lost his shoe in the middle of the show! However, he got the black loafer back on his foot midsong without missing a beat.

One of the funniest things I remember from the Victory tour was listening to Knoxville radio station WIMZ-FM as they celebrated "Jacksons Day" weekend, complete with a countdown to "Jacksons Eve," on-the-air conversations about putting up a "Jacksons Tree," hanging the "Jacksons Stockings" on the fireplace, and the traditional singing of "Jacksons Carols" like that old favorite "Have Yourself A Merry Little Concert!" For Knoxville, Tennessee, Christmas had come in August—in the form of Michael Jackson!

Even with the death threats, the temporary concert postponement, the rain on Friday night, and all the extra added confusion, all three of the Knoxville concerts proved a roaring success. The next stop on the agenda was Detroit, Michigan, better known in music circles as Motown!

CHAPTER TEN

RETURN TO MOTOWN

"We love you, Motown!" shouted Michael Jackson to the Motor City crowd from on stage at the Pontiac Silverdome, and the ultra-enthusiastic Detroit crowd gave back their love to the gloved one in the form of thunderous nonstop cheering, screaming, and applauding for three solid nights of thrills as the Jacksons showed Motown what Victory was all about.

It had been fifteen years since Michael Jackson and the Jackson Five recorded their first number-one hit, "I Want You Back," in downtown Detroit for Motown Records. When the Jacksons played the Detroit area on August 17, 18, and 19, 1984, it was like a homecoming celebration!

Now, I don't want to be accused of being at all biased, but the audiences at the Silverdome in my hometown of Pontiac, Michigan, were without a doubt the best, most responsive, most exciting and demonstrative crowds on the entire tour! Not since the Beatles in 1964 has there been such pop-idol hysteria as that which Michael Jackson inspires, and to borrow a current inner-city phrase, in those three concerts, Motown "threw down"! That weekend in Pontiac, it was one big party.

Michael himself was so impressed with the shows' reception at the Silverdome that there were rumors of the Victory tour doing an encore in Pontiac later in the fall.

Gary Graff of the *Detroit Free Press* asked me to do an article on the Victory tour for the August 16, 1984, edition as a guest editorial. Since I grew up in the Detroit suburbs, I've always considered myself a native Detroiter, so it was a big treat for me to write a piece for the top daily newspaper in the Motor City.

Having just been through the Knoxville fiasco, my article ended with, "So, if you're a jaded skeptic or a troublemaker, stay away from the Silverdome this weekend. You're unwanted. But, if you believe in escapism, fantasy, Peter Pan, sizzling rock music and a trust that the American Dream is still something that can be attained, then do not miss Michael Jackson—he is living proof of all of the above."

Meanwhile, the plans for the concerts in metropolitan Detroit were the most mixed-up bookings in the tour's short history. First it had been announced that Michael and his brothers would play at the Silverdome on August 25 and 26, then the word was that they would be scheduled for the weekend before, August 18 and 19, as well. Then it was announced that the show would occur only on August 18 and 19. Then, only days before the weekend, Friday, August 17, was added as well. In addition, a rumor was circulating that, due to the cancellation of the Los Angeles Forum dates planned for September and the death threats in Knoxville, the Victory tour might end on the second night this weekend, with a worldwide live satellite TV simulcast grand finale. The performances were finally locked in for Friday, Saturday, and Sunday, August 17 to 19. But, to top it all off, the Silverdome contracts were signed only hours before the gates opened for Friday's concert!

Rumors among us journalists covering the tour suggested that, due to the fall football season, Chuck Sullivan was running into serious problems booking the tour. It was evident that the tour schedule was being thrown together on such short notice that there could be serious problems selling out all the shows. (In fact, there were unsold tickets for Friday night in Detroit, and for both Buffalo shows the following weekend.) By this point it was crystal clear that when it came to concert scheduling, only one thing could be expected from the Victory tour—and that was the unexpected!

At the concerts in Pontiac, the crowd ran the gamut from T-shirts to tuxedos. The audiences were absolutely the most enthusiastic of the entire tour, and nonstop clapping and screaming accompanied every song. Only the intensity of the cheers fluctuated.

Keeping with the family-audience theme that the entire tour elicited, on Friday night in Pontiac I took my mother to see Michael Jackson in action, and my sister Anne went with me on Saturday. When questioned as to whether she'd have preferred to sit in one of the glassed-in boxes at the Silverdome or not, my mom shot back, "Are you kidding, and miss all the excitement of the crowd down here? No, thank you. This is a 'happening,' being part of the mob!"

The Pontiac Silverdome was another unique venue for the Jacksons. Its full capacity is 80,000, and although it is built like an open-air stadium, it has a nylon weather-resistant roof that is suspended by the force of air currents pumped into it. Hence, even on hot summer nights, it remains comfortable.

Detroit audiences, especially for rock and roll acts, are known for being boisterous and wild—and this engagement was no exception. But like the rest of the Victory concerts, the audiences all three nights were orderly, and composed mostly of young fans and their families. The sound quality was a bit muddy on Friday night, due to too much echo off the roof. Saturday night the sound was much better and the audience reactions even more vivid. On Sunday night the show was sold out at a capacity of 49,200, including many obstructed-view seats behind the light tower. The third night in Pontiac, I had a very different perspective on the concert, which I recorded in my notebook that night as it happened.

JOURNAL ENTRY—SUNDAY, AUGUST 19, 1984

It is 9:18 P.M. on Sunday, August 19, 1984, and I am sitting in the second to last row in the uppermost balcony of the Pontiac Silverdome, jokingly known on this tour as "the nosebleed section." I have been curious to sit on this level to see what the visual vantage point is like from the least desirable and furthermost point from the stage. The show tonight is a total sellout. In fact, all the extra seats that went on sale today described as "obstructed-view" seats have also completely sold out. My seat tonight is comparable to sitting on the roof of an eight-story building a block away, looking down.

It is 9:32 P.M., and suddenly the lights go down. As I look down at the crowd, I see a dark sea dotted with flickering matches and lit cigarette lighters. As Randy pulls the sword from the stone and the lasers shoot upward to the domed ceiling, it is impressive from up here to see the brilliance of the colored light beams.

Although they are absolutely minute from up here, the Jacksons are still dramatic as they rise up out of the floor of the stage. People around me eagerly take turns with shared binoculars. Even through powerful binoculars, at this distance the Jacksons are a fraction of an inch tall! And although he appears small enough to moonwalk on the head of a pin, Michael Jackson's glittering glove and sequined socks are still readable to the naked eye.

As the lights aiming down at the stage swivel downstage to illuminate the entire audience, from this height it is a real rush to see 49,200 people screaming and squealing in ecstasy amid "Wanna Be Startin' Something."

The band appears to be seated atop microchips from a computer memory bank, but the lights, the music, and the excitement still carry all the way up to this level— as far away from Michael as one can get and still be in the Silverdome!

As the laser beams shoot up to us at the end of the song "Off The Wall," there is a strange sort of continuum between us and the superstar ants on the stage down below.

From up here I can see why the video screen is such an integral part of the show—even with binoculars it is impossible to get the facial close-ups it provides. The excitement does carry! Again, as proven in the past two nights Detroit audiences are the absolute best when it comes to rock concerts. Enthusiasm plus!

When the tiny figure of Michael Jackson reappears on stage to join Jermaine on "Tell Me I'm Not Dreamin' (Too Good To Be True)," the people around me flip out with their cheering. Even from up here, these folks know a thriller when they see one, even if he seems to be a quarter of a mile away! In the middle of the song, one of the cameramen who is traveling with the Jacksons rushes up the aisle next to me to capture this view on tape for Michael's video of the tour. A video cassette and/or a TV special is inevitable. In the middle of the Motown medley, the bearded video cameraman sits down on the step next to me and shoots the sequence as well as getting footage of the cheering crowd.

People nearly fall off their seats for "Billie Jean" as minuscule Michael moonwalks backward an acre away from where I sit. To see him excite so many people is a real rush. The stage is his and he works it to death!

As the band slides into "Shake Your Body (Down To The Ground)," it is absolutely riveting to see 49,200 people swinging their arms to the music. This is the twentieth time I have seen this show, and the concert still has my eyes glued to the stage.

Since Michael Jackson first found fame at Motown Records in 1969, we native Detroiters feel as if he is a hometown boy—and tonight Detroit really showed him how we feel about him. Michael got so excited at the end of the show that he threw his black sequined "Billie Jean" jacket into the audience, to become the prize of some lucky fan!

DETROIT DEVELOPMENTS

According to *Billboard* magazine, in the three Detroit dates the Jacksons sold 145,000 tickets and grossed $4,350,030. Over four million dollars! Not bad for one weekend.

On the third night of concerts at the Silverdome, over forty disadvantaged children from Michael's hometown of Gary, Indiana, were the group's special guests in the audience. Since all negotiations had fallen through to play the Gary-Chicago area, the Jacksons paid all expenses to rent a bus and bring them to Detroit to see the concert there. Accompanied by Dr. Vernon Smith, head of Gary's City Council, and family friend from Gary, Marcus Fairchild, the children came from the Thelma Marshall Children's Home for orphans, foster children, and abandoned children; the Hoosier Boys' Home; and the Donzels Work-Study Program for high school students working toward a college education. Since the Jacksons couldn't get to Gary, they simply brought a little bit of Gary to them!

"Where is Michael staying?" was one of the most asked questions in each city of the tour. Fans hounded Anatole's hotel in Dallas so much that Michael took off and spent three days with his friend—former child star Spanky McFarland of the original "Our Gang" movies. Michael's Detroit whereabouts leaked out when it was discovered that he was staying at the Somerset Inn in Troy, Michigan. Even after the frightening Knoxville fiasco, surprisingly, a number of Detroit-area fans ended up with handshakes and autographs.

On Sunday afternoon of the Jacksons' weekend in Detroit, a group of Jackson fans in the parking lot of the Somerset Inn spelled out the word "Hi" with their bodies in the parking lot and got Jermaine's attention. Jermaine rewarded them with a wave from his window. Michael's $192 per night penthouse suite was not easy to reach without clearance. However, some persistently sly admirers got through to "M.J." himself!

Eleven-year-old Ryan Dembs somehow found the direct-dial telephone number to Michael's suite. When he reached the startled star on the phone, Michael astonishingly said, "You're the only one who has my room number!" Ryan was invited up to meet Michael and get an autograph. Said Ryan when asked how he got the number, "That's a secret!"

Catherine Waldbatt, twenty-one, wangled her way to Michael's suite just ten minutes before he slipped out of the Somerset Inn through a rear exit. Michael, who never once removed his dark glasses during their encounter, shook Catherine's hand, thanked her for a pillow she had made for him, and autographed a photo for her. Catherine said, "He was very polite and spoke very softly. I initiated all conversation. He just responded to everything I said. He didn't smile at all. In fact, he looked very artificial. I didn't know it was him until he spoke, and his hand was ice cold."

As Michael left via the delivery entrance of the hotel at 1:45 P.M., sixteen-year-old Julie Wechesler was standing there waiting, even though the majority of the fans were waiting out front. Julie said, "I wanted a picture and his autograph, but I was able to shake his hand. There's so many people who didn't even get to meet him!"

MICHAEL MEETS THE POLICE

The *Pontiac* police force, that is! My father mentioned to me that he regularly golfed with someone from the Pontiac Police Department, who mentioned that Michael Jackson had been at the Pontiac City Hall with a troop of police officers. Michael's cameramen had filmed them escorting him down the steps and into a police car. According to the source, Captain Robert Burns had organized the video shooting upon Michael's request, so I called the police department and spoke to Burns to find out the details.

Burns said, "I was approached by his production manager, Patrick Kelly, Saturday evening. Actually, he'd approached one of my lieutenants earlier, but I finally got in touch with Patrick on Saturday. They wanted to do a skit in the tunnel underneath the Silverdome, and we suggested that perhaps it might be better to do it at the police station; be more convenient for Michael, rather than doing it just prior to the show, and it would be more convenient for us, because my people at the Silverdome have other assignments. So we worked out an arrangement where they were going to do it on Sunday afternoon, and we did it around six o'clock here at the police department."

With regard to the scenario of Michael's video footage, Captain Burns explained, "We had the officers line up, and they took photographs of them in three columns, Michael leading the center column. They jogged down the back steps to a waiting police car, and Michael jumped in the police car and sped off."

"As though he was the police commissioner being ushered down into the car by the police?" I asked.

"Yes," said Burns, who added, "They were there I guess about forty minutes or so. They did two run-throughs of that, and they had the officers put on pairs of black glasses like Michael wears, and they did a walk down the steps and to the police car again. They did one run-through on that one."

Still convinced that a Victory tour video cassette was inevitable, I asked Captain Burns if he was told what specifically the footage was going to be used for, to which he replied, "Michael's personal home movies, as far as I'm told."

THE JACKSONS IN THE NEWS

During the week the Jacksons were conquering the Silverdome audiences in Michigan, they were all over the headlines, together and individually.

The four days between their concerts in Knoxville and Detroit, all six Jackson brothers got together at the famous Kaufman Astoria Studios in Queens, New York, to film a video of the song "Torture," which was the second single to be released from the *Victory* album. The video was lensed by Picture Music and was directed by Jeff Stein, executive-produced by John Diaz, and produced by T'boo Dalton. However, in the middle of the production, Michael apparently had a disagreement with his brothers. Reported the *New York Daily News* in its August 22 edition, "A tiff—nature unknown—broke out between Michael and the brothers and, say our sources, a wax dummy of Michael had to serve as a stand-in for the genuine gloved article on the set." Upon further investigation, I found out that Michael was so upset that he took off for the nearest place that he could compose himself: Disney World! Originally I had been invited onto the set of the video to cover the shooting, but the offer was rescinded after the problems among the Jacksons broke out.

The same article in the *Daily News* went on to say that Michael had had recent meetings regarding his forthcoming film career. Jackson was said to be out at the East Hampton home of Warner Communications head Steve Ross, where he was joined by Quincy Jones and Steven Spielberg. The conversation that ensued regarded a major new motion picture project for Michael, and it would not be the new version of *Peter Pan* that had been discussed previously. The article outlined the fact that Michael would star in it, Quincy would score the soundtrack, Steven would direct, Warner would produce, and Epic Records would release the original soundtrack album. Sounded like a sure-fire hit to me!

Also that week came the news that Sigmund (Jackie) Jackson's wife, Enid, was suing him for divorce. An article in the August 22 issue of *Variety* stated that Enid was seeking one-half of Jackie's earnings from the Victory tour, plus $53,000 a month for child support for herself!

Another article in the August 22 *Variety* was titled "Jacksons Suddenly Redo Buffalo Concert Dates; No Immediate Sellout." The sudden schedule changes in the Victory tour were described and cited as the reason for a slowdown in ticket sales. It had been anticipated that both Saturday and Sunday's concerts in Buffalo would sell out, and a Friday show would be added to make up for the demand, but ultimately there were leftover tickets for both weekend dates, and no third show was even called for. *Variety* called the changes "a move that caught many of their fans with their bucks down." The article also stated that "not only were the fans caught short, but local Pepsi-Cola distributors did not have sufficient time to fire up a cooperative campaign with the superstars their company is helping to promote."

In the same *Variety* was the news that a man in Mount Vernon, New York, had been arrested for selling bootleg video cassettes of the July 6 opening night Victory concert from Kansas City. The tape was made illegally by tapping into the closed-circuit multicamera signal from the video feed to the giant screen above the stage.

In the August 21 issue of *USA Today* came word that in Memphis, Tennessee—at the Orpheum Theater on August 31—would be the opening of the ninety-minute stage show titled *Thriller of a Lifetime*. You guessed it—it's a live stage musical based on the life of Michael Jackson! The August 23 edition of the same newspaper carried the news that the Hollywood Chamber of Commerce had decided where to place the Michael Jackson star on the Hollywood Boulevard Walk of Fame. The spot: right in front of Mann's Chinese Theater, where the movie stars have for years immortalized their handprints and footprints in the cement.

On August 26 an item ran in the *Detroit Free Press* saying that American music was alive and well in Soviet Russia—on the black market, that is. Michael Jackson albums, it seems, were currently available under the table for a cost of up to one hundred rubles ($130) each! The music of the Beatles and Elvis Presley followed closely to Michael's in being hot items in that illegal market. Radio Russia complained about Jackson-mania, "Have we really nothing with which to counter this whole dirty wave?"

As you can see, Jackson-mania had yet to peak. In fact, it continued to grow and grow. The same week that all this news broke, newsstands across America unwrapped bundles of the latest Michael Jackson cover story—this time in the

September 1984 issue of prestigious *Life* magazine.

During this same period, Michael had two very successful competitors for concert ticket sales and for record sales: Bruce Springsteen and his *Born In The U.S.A.* tour and album, and Prince, with his movie soundtrack from *Purple Rain*.

THE VICTORY ALBUM

The week the Jacksons rolled into Detroit was a very significant one for them on the American record charts. According to the August 18, 1984, issue of *Billboard* magazine, there were three Jackson hits on the "Hot 100" singles chart, and five Jackson LPs on the album chart.

The Jacksons' single "State Of Shock" held the number-3 spot on the singles chart, while Jermaine's "Dynamite" was climbing at number 24. That week saw the chart debut of the Jacksons' single "Torture" at number 48. On the album chart *Victory* was number 4, having peaked at number 3. Also on the charts were Michael's albums *Thriller* (number 31), *Farewell My Summer Love* (number 105), and *Off The Wall* (number 111). *Thriller* was in its 87th consecutive week on the album charts, while "Off The Wall" was in its 162nd charted week! The *Jermaine Jackson* album also made the top 40.

Oddly enough, the *Victory* album was not selling as well as originally anticipated. In the next couple of weeks, it would fall to number seven and number nine without even being certified gold. Prince and his *Purple Rain* album had the number-one slot sewn up for this entire period, while "Ghostbusters" by Ray Parker, Jr., and "When Doves Cry" by Prince dominated the number-one slot on the singles chart. In the British album charts, Michael's *Thriller* was holding strong at number seven while *Victory* fell to a dismal number seventeen.

Personally, I've always liked the *Victory* album, and feel very strongly that it is the best total album that the Jacksons as a group have done to date on Epic Records. All of the cuts on the album are very good, and the three songs featuring Michael's lead singing are all excellent. Each of the three Michael songs on the album are completely different in tone and feeling.

There is no question that this album is a patchwork quilt of eight different songs, each written and produced and sung by different Jackson brothers or different combinations of Jackson brothers. On two of the cuts, members of the Grammy Award-winning rock group Toto serve as co-writers and co-producers. Other than their presence, there is no single producing influence unifying the project. In fact, the brothers were mainly working in different recording studios at different times, and when it came time to pick the songs that would comprise the album, the elements were then stitched together into the eight-song LP that bears the name *Victory*. Oddly, there is no song titled "Victory" on the disk.

In terms of creativity, energy, and musical excitement, the best cut on the album is "Torture," which opens side one. It is a sparkling up-tempo duet between Jermaine and Michael Jackson, with all six brothers on the background vocals. The song was produced and composed by Jackie Jackson, with lyrics by Jackie and co-writer Kathy Wakefield.

Beginning with a pounding bass guitar and soaring synthesizer intro, "Torture" has crisp percussion embellishments fluttering from speaker to speaker as the cut simmers toward a sweeping crescendo. With weeping guitar riffs behind his voice, Jermaine begins his narrative singing about the advice that a mysterious and psychic lady gives him about life and love. The six Jackson brothers chime in like an ethereal choir, harmonizing that life without love is "torture."

Michael takes the lead and describes how he follows the vampy medium up a staircase to a secluded room, where she offers to fulfill his every desire. Trading off choruses, Michael and Jermaine feel like they've awakened from a dream. Was she flesh or fantasy? Either way it's "torture!" the brothers concur in the background with harmonious sibling savvy. The song is smooth rock and roll, and it is an obvious choice for a hit single. This is the album's big ensemble piece, with all the brothers working as a unit. From this point in the album on, it is seven solo showcases. "Torture" is mainly carried by the group's choral singing, while Jack Wargo's guitar solo provides a gliding instrumental bridge into the exciting crescendo finale.

"Wait" is Jackie's turn in the solo-singing spotlight. Produced by Jackie and Toto members David Paich and Jeff Porcaro, the song is a percolating synthesizer-laden rocker with supportive choral and solo scatting by Michael and the guys. The pace is slick and peppy, and Jackie shows off his glorious falsetto to full advantage. Paich and Jackie Jackson wrote this song about an impatient lover's plea.

"One More Chance" is a beautiful showcase for youngest Jackson brother Randy. His voice glides atop a cloud of lush and romantic keyboards. The love song about lovers making up after a quarrel is a mellow and soothing ballad that suggests the next logical candidate for a solo Jacksons album is Randy.

"Be Not Always" is without a doubt one of the most beautiful and touching ballads that Michael Jackson has ever sung. Crooning to the delicate sound of a lone acoustic guitar, Michael is joined by a harp and viola for a classic baroque sound. When a sea of concert violinists join in, it is indeed a moving and sentimental message song straight from Michael, and dealing with mortality and the tragic reality of fate. Composed by Michael, with additional lyrics by Marlon, the poignant ballad is as meaningful and inspiring as the best of Emily Dickinson's poetry. The sound quality is sharp, and Michael's deeply felt emotions about man's inhumanity to man come quivering through loud and clear. The song is the inspirational highlight on the album.

The next song on *Victory* takes the mood 180 degrees in the opposite direction—to the outrageous Michael Jackson-Mick Jagger duet, "State Of Shock." The whole composition is clearly constructed as a tongue-in-cheek tribute to the Rolling Stones' hard-hitting trademark rock and roll sound. Both Michael and Mick work overtime to put on their best Mick Jagger impersonations within the slapping and driving rock number. M.J. and M.J. match each other in a vocal duel of mugging and bantering back and forth for the affections of a shockingly desirable young lady. It's almost like the hard-rock version of "The Girl Is Mine," and a real campy cult classic of a hit.

Tito takes the lead vocal microphone for the bouncy and progressive message song "We Can Change The World." Tito plays the majority of the keyboards on this smooth, midtempo and jazzy rock ballad, with Louis Johnson of the Brothers Johnson providing the bass line. Take it, Tito! A surprisingly good solo debut from a Jackson brother we've never heard on his own.

Likewise, "The Hurt" is Randy's chance to compose, do keyboards, and sing lead in his highest register as he wrestles with more of the agonies of love. All six brothers sing background, giving us falsetto to the max! Co-produced by the Jacksons and Toto stars Paich and Porcaro, the song is another solid showcase for Randy as a singer and a musician in his own right. Randy and Michael wrote the tune with Paich and Porcaro.

The album ends with Marlon's entry into this ultimate Jackson family album. Marlon's composition "Body" is a snappy and steamy cross between "Can You Feel It" and "Shake Your Body (Down To The Ground)." The song deals with carnal fires and desires, to the tune of "I want your body" and "I need your body." Definitely a direct approach for breaking the ice! Marlon shows off his stylish and soulful vocal wares.

Throughout the *Victory* album, the production quality and singing is stamped with the professionalism of people who have been producing hit records for fifteen years. Each cut is a quest to break new ground and become an ensemble of six talented individuals, not just Michael Jackson's family background group. Every brother has his place in the sun on this album, and the group concept is successfully stretched in many new directions. It will be interesting to see where they go from here as a recording group. *Victory* never intends to be the follow-up to Michael's *Thriller* but should be viewed as a strong follow-up to the Jacksons' last group studio LP, 1980's *Triumph*. *Victory* is not a landmark in modern music, but a quirky sampler of very diverse and consistently good songs from the individual Jackson brothers: Jermaine, Tito, Randy, Marlon, Jackie, and family superstar, Michael.

Victory was released as a record album, a cassette, a compact disk, and a special picture disk with the science-fiction-looking cover portrait of the Jacksons pressed into clear plastic for the serious Jackson collector.

CHAPTER ELEVEN

SHUFFLING OFF TO BUFFALO... AND PHILADELPHIA

Was it a Michael Jackson backlash or was it the hasty last-minute tour planning? Or was it the false announcement that there would be a third Victory concert that week? Whatever the reason, on Wednesday, August 22, approximately 38,000 tickets remained unsold for the two weekend concerts in Buffalo, New York.

"I'm boycotting the Jacksons' concert," a Philadelphia radio interviewer told me, "because I feel that the public has been manipulated!" As the *Buffalo News* pointed out, "By now, you're either sick of hearing about Michael Jackson or dying to hear more. There seems to be no middle ground."

The concerts in Buffalo were announced only a week before they took place, and the economically depressed city was clearly torn. While there were many unsold tickets when the show started on Saturday night, some fans had camped out for over twenty-five hours in front of ticket-selling outlets to buy choice seats. To top that off, every single limousine in the area had been rented. Local limousine companies were turning down several customers an hour.

What was happening was clearly a case of the big-business machinery of the modern-day entertainment world hurting Michael Jackson's career. While Michael was still being acknowledged as a highly talented and creative individual, people were responding negatively to the dealings of the tour-planning organization.

It was obvious that Michael and the brothers had better conjure up a little public relations magic real soon. From Buffalo on, in each city they visited, a pilgrimage to the local children's hospitals was made by Marlon, Tito, and/or Randy. Stadium Management Corporation was also handing out tickets to charities in each of the cities at an average of four hundred per show. Pepsi-Cola as well was very active in donating tickets to charity.

By this point in the tour, although Michael refused to speak to any members of the press, I was slowly but surely finding out bits and pieces of tour gossip. Whenever anything Jackson related would happen, someone would call me. Various people connected with the tour were taking me aside and telling me different episodes and various fascinating items of information.

Here's an example: Many times during the tour I had seen a certain gentleman on airplanes, at concerts, and at Jackson-related functions. When I inquired about him to one of my sources, I was informed that the man in question was a sort of liaison to the black communities on the tour. When I asked what his exact purpose was, my source informed me that "Mr. X" basically did nothing, but had threatened to create trouble in the form of racist allegations, and so was bought off with free tickets to the whole tour. I was finally beginning to realize how complicated the inner workings of the tour actually were.

At 9:50 P.M. on Saturday night it looked to me like Buffalo's Rich Stadium was quite full, although there were some conspicuously empty seats in the uppermost areas. It was a perfectly clear and slightly cool evening. The show was, as usual, tight and slick. The audience was excited by Michael's every move. Juggler Chris Bliss, however, didn't fare so well. In fact, the crowd gave him quite a strong round of booing the minute he took the stage. For them anything less than M.J. simply wouldn't do.

In the middle of "She's Out Of My Life," someone in the audience threw a bouquet of red roses to Michael on stage. He knelt down, picked them up while continuing to sing, and then tossed them to the crowd. Throughout the Buffalo concerts the sound quality was very good, with each of the individual musical instruments sounding very crisp.

As I sat in Rich Stadium that night and watched the crowd getting into Jermaine's new hit, "Dynamite," I realized what a big mistake it was for the Jacksons not to perform a single song from their album *Victory*. I kept expecting them to add something from it in the show, but it never happened. This was the week that the *Victory* album had begun to slip on the sales charts in America. It seemed so odd that "Torture" was never given a live presentation.

The way the Jacksons' stage was set up in Rich Stadium made the capacity of salable seats 48,200. On Saturday the audience totaled 47,000 tickets sold, and on Sunday the figure was just over 47,000. Neither show sold out, and tickets were available right up until show time. "We think over forty-seven thousand is a terrific crowd, we're very pleased with Buffalo," said Chuck Sullivan, who added, "The souvenir sales were dynamite. From what we're hearing, the sales in Buffalo are the best on the tour!" Although falling short of a sellout was hardly a major problem, it was again strange that the demand wasn't greater, especially when Sullivan was prepared to have added a Friday show had the ticket sales been there. The hot interest in the show seemed to be cooling off.

CHARITABLE CAUSES

With all the negative publicity that some aspects of the tour were generating, the Jacksons were progressively balancing the scales by making some highly publicized charitable gestures in each of the cities that they visited.

On Sunday, August 26, I was present at the Children's

Hospital of Buffalo when Marlon Jackson, on behalf of the Jacksons and Pepsi-Cola, donated a refrigerator to the seventh-floor playroom of the institution. The refrigerator, by the way, was filled with special Jacksons commemorative cans of Pepsi.

The presentation was scheduled to take place at one in the afternoon. By five minutes to one, the main lobby of the hospital was filled with young patients, orderlies wearing green surgical scrub uniforms, doctors with stethoscopes around their necks, and kids of all ages armed with autograph books and wearing Jacksons buttons. Those in the crowd were climbing over each other for a glimpse of the superstar Jackson brother.

It was well after 1:30 when a beige Chevy van with a plush blue interior pulled up at the hospital. Out stepped Marlon, dressed in a shiny but conservative grayish-brown suit and mirror sunglasses. The whole entourage of bodyguards, TV cameramen, reporters, and photographers jammed into three waiting elevators, and we were whisked off to the seventh floor. The throng of fans in the lobby was held back by security guards and not allowed off the main floor.

When we got to the seventh-floor playroom, the scene was one of utter chaos. People were pushing and shoving to get better camera angles. One of the TV cameramen knocked my tape recorder out of my hand and onto the floor. The next thing I knew I was pinned up against an electronic hockey game. Little kids with intravenous needles sticking out of their arms were jostled and pushed about by overly eager cameramen looking for that perfect shot.

Amid the craziness, a calm and composed Marlon signed plaster casts and obligingly autographed all that was put before him. He also posed for dozens of pictures while holding small children. One little boy named Matthew looked terrified as Marlon held him and they were hit by thousands of watts of flashbulb light.

While signing "Love, Marlon Jackson" on everything in sight, Michael's older brother never once removed his dark glasses. He looked oblivious to the confusion that was going on around him. With the sounds of small children crying and the behavior of the rudely aggressive photographers pushing and shoving for better camera angles, the scene was that of a three-ring circus. After presenting the Pepsi-filled refrigerator, Marlon went on to visit some of the intensive-care patients. I shuddered to think of the scene that would have ensued had Michael himself shown up. One hundred Jacksons T-shirts were handed out, and Marlon next went on to Ronald McDonald House, which boards families of sick children being treated at the hospital, where he signed more autographs.

At the show that night, although the air was a bit cool, the crowd was decidedly hot. A little girl sitting next to me was absolutely in tears over Michael's "She's Out Of My Life." The sentimental ballad brought uncontrollable fits of weeping from her. "What's wrong? What's wrong?" the young teenager's father asked in a concerned tone. "I love Michael!" the girl sobbed in simultaneous agony and ecstasy at seeing the gloved one perform before her eyes.

Including Buffalo, New York, in the first two months of the Victory tour, a record total of 1.1 million tickets had been sold. In 1982 the rock group Styx tallied over a million tickets sold—but it took them seven months to do it. The Jacksons accomplished well over a million tickets sold during July and August alone! And Victory was next to roll into September with three Labor Day weekend dates in Philadelphia, Pennsylvania.

MICHAEL'S TWENTY-SIXTH BIRTHDAY

On Wednesday, August 29, 1984, Michael Jackson turned twenty-six years old. As a Jehovah's Witness, Michael did nothing special to mark the occasion. It seems that members of that religion do not commemorate birthdays or observe Christmas. No birthday cakes or formal acknowledgments marked any of the Victory concerts—with the exception of my spotting some "Happy Birthday Michael" banners in the audience in Detroit and Buffalo.

Speaking of the Jehovah's Witnesses, in addition to the fact that some members of the church are appalled by Michael's "Thriller" video and flamboyant stage persona, there is also a sect of Witnesses that believes Jackson is in actuality the Archangel Michael returned to earth!

PHILADELPHIA, PENNSYLVANIA

On Wednesday, August 22, it was announced that the Jacksons' Victory tour would be playing in Philadelphia on Labor Day weekend—September 1, 2, and 3. Originally the Philadelphia concerts were planned for October 5 and 6, but in the ongoing Victory confusion, this last-minute change was par for the course, and tickets went on sale August 23. With such late planning, none of the three concerts ended up being total sellouts. Despite the available tickets, Stadium Management Corporation did not purchase a single inch of advertising space to announce or move the tickets. As in all the cities on the tour, they relied unwisely on word of mouth to herald Michael's arrival at each venue. This resulted in many unsold tickets, and in Buffalo and Denver, options on third-night shows were never picked up due to poor initial sales.

When I arrived in town in time to appear on the TV show *AM Philadelphia*, the first question I was asked on the air was "They're talking about adding Mick Jagger to the program, I think because ticket sales aren't going well. [Do] you have some insight in that?" I had to cite a Jagger quote that ran in the September 13 issue of *Rolling Stone* which read, "Anyone who thinks I'd travel 3000 miles to sing a song for five minutes is out of his mind!" Mick was in England and had no intention of crossing the Atlantic Ocean to embellish someone else's concert—not even Michael Jackson's.

JFK Stadium in Philadelphia is fifty-eight years old and

pretty tired looking. The hard, backless bleachers that the majority of the audience sat in are made of fiberglass that is so badly worn that tiny fiberglass slivers stick to your hands if you touch them. Jacksons publicist Neil Friedman laughed that "this stadium reminds me of the kind in South America where they take political prisoners!"

The Victory dates at JFK Stadium were the Woodstock concerts of the tour—no balconies, no tiers, just a sea of 60,000 faces spread out around the stage. Seated on the sloping bleachers or chairs on the field, these concerts had the seats farthest from the stage.

Saturday night's show attracted both Bruce Springsteen and Sly Stone, and one of the largest audiences on the entire tour. The sound was quite clear and its quality very good, but most of those in the Philadelphia audience really needed to watch the image on the projection screen to follow the action. When people began waving their arms in the air to "I'll Be There," it was really quite a sight—120,000 arms swaying to Michael's hypnotic crooning. This audience was very much into participation—they sang and clapped during "Rock With You," and at long last a crowd chanted "We want more! We want more! We want more!" at the false exit after "Lovely One." That moment had so often been met with dumbfounded silence. Everything that cool Saturday night worked perfectly.

On Sunday, September 2, Andy Hernandez (a.k.a. Coati Mundi) of the rock group Kid Creole and the Coconuts came down to Philly to visit and catch the show. That night, for one reason or another many people in the audience close to the stage tossed bouquets of fresh flowers to Michael during the show. During "She's Out Of My Life," Michael posed midsong with a bunch of red roses that had been tossed at his feet.

When I asked Andy what he thought of the show, we discussed the fact that this was going to be Michael's last concert tour with the brothers, and the significance of that. Andy said, "As a performer who believes in injecting high energy into a show, I can appreciate more than most what goes into the making of a Michael Jackson performance. The dictionary should contain another word that means 'great, superb, professional, energetic, entertaining,' and that word should be 'michaeljackson.' As far as the Jacksons in general, I appreciate their efforts to grow as performers. Tito has some way to go with the guitar, but he is trying. Randy is the best musician and should be a star in his own right. Jermaine is hanging real tough as a bass player and has a good voice. Marlon is a good dancer and has great theatrical attitude. Personally, I would rather see Michael Jackson continuing to perform with his brothers than on the stage alone."

THE "TORTURE" VIDEO

On Monday, September 3, it was Labor Day, and at 7:00 P.M. the Jacksons' "Torture" video had its debut on the music television station MTV. The real shocker was that neither Michael nor Jermaine had anything to do with the video and do not appear in it, even though it is the two of them who sing the lead vocals on the song!

The video's plot is like that of a science-fiction movie, with Jackie Jackson being attacked by a bunch of scantily clad girls dressed as spiders. Tito, Randy, and Marlon dance through it while being pursued by exotic women from space. The video also includes five break-dancing skeletons who also mimic Jackson Five choreography. There is no question that as the camera pans five still figures of the brothers (sans Jermaine) what we see is a wax dummy of Michael posed with his four brothers. The other ploy to suggest Michael's image is a couple of frames of a sequined glove grabbing the end of a whip. Other than the dummy and the stand-in hand, Michael is nowhere to be found. It almost gives the impression that Michael said to his brothers: "I sang on your record—now do your own video."

When I tried to reach several people at Epic Records for the inside story, they refused to comment. When I called

Jermaine's label, Kenneth Reynolds from Arista Records said that he had been informed that Jermaine and Michael were expected to be in the video, but when he received a phone call from Jermaine, Reynolds learned that Jermaine was in Los Angeles, while Randy, Tito, Marlon, and Jackie were in New York City filming "Torture." As I stated earlier, this same week Michael went to Disney World instead. However, no one would or could explain to me why the "Torture" video features only four Jacksons.

RAINY DAYS AND MONDAYS

On Monday, September 3, it began to rain at 5:30 in the afternoon. The rain swiftly became a torrential downpour, complete with hailstones. It subsided for a couple of hours, but by 8:00 the rains again claimed the skies. By the time I pulled my car into the parking lot at JFK Stadium, it was 9:00 P.M. and the rain continued to fall steadily.

When I got up to the stadium, there were long lines of wet people waiting to get inside, but all the gates were closed. Inside the small enclosed area within the gates were thousands of people trying to stay dry. As I questioned a guard, I found out that it still hadn't been determined whether or not the concert was going to be postponed or would indeed take place at all. It was clear that the crowd was completely prepared to sit outside in the rain and get soaking wet— anything just to see Michael Jackson.

At 9:34 on my watch, it was announced that the show had definitely been canceled. "There is no rain date!" a security guard shouted to me through the gates when I asked what the policy was going to be as far as rescheduling. When the gates were opened up, some very disappointed fans poured out of the stadium. Kids crying and parents complaining were common sights that night in "Mudville." It seemed crazy not to have scheduled a single rain date for any of the cities booked on the tour. Didn't the concert promoters expect that in five months of touring in outdoor arenas it would rain at last once? Mother Nature takes a pause for no one's concert tour—not even Michael Jackson's. The stage had to be dismantled and reassembled 1,691 miles away in Denver, Colorado, by Friday night, so there was no way the concert could be rescheduled and held in Philadelphia the following night.

One of the people who waited in the rain and got wet along with the rest of us was Pennsylvania Senator James Lloyd. According to him, "You should have seen the acute disappointment on the faces of those kids when they found out the show would not be rescheduled. This was a multimillion-dollar tour, yet they did not plan well enough to protect the consumer and schedule a rain date." The Victory show getting rained out that night caused Senator Lloyd to introduce a bill on the floor of the state senate to require all outdoor concerts to have rain dates scheduled from this point on.

Despite the disappointment of his fans, no one that night in any way blamed Michael Jackson for the concert's not taking place. In fact, the gloved wonder never even left his hotel that night. It was evident that something had to be done to clear up the negative feelings of over 50,000 ticket-holding fans who gathered in Philadelphia that Labor Day but were asked to "beat it." A lot of people had come from out of town just to see their hero moonwalk, and all they got was wet feet.

By 5:00 P.M. the next day a scheduled 2:00 press conference had still not taken place to announce the plans for refunds or rescheduling. In the end, an additional Philadelphia weekend was added to the schedule for September 28 and 29 so that the City of Brotherly Love could feel the same way about the Jacksons and their tour. For people holding tickets that night who could not make it back to Philadelphia at the end of September, there were no refunds. Talk about a raw deal for out-of-towners!

HIS HOTNESS

On the cover of the September 4, 1984, edition of the *Philadelphia Daily News*, there was a huge portrait of Michael singing in concert, and the headline over the top of it read simply "His Hotness." The term was quite apt, because about this same time, stores across the country were debuting the "Official Michael Jackson Calendar" for 1985. Among the many photos of him was one in which he is seated on a throne wearing a shiny bejeweled crown. His Highness, Michael Joseph Jackson, the Crown Prince Of Pop, was now officially dubbed "His Hotness"!

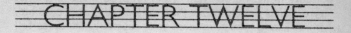

CHAPTER TWELVE

MILE HIGH AND MONTREAL

It was at the post-show press briefing on Saturday night in
Buffalo that Victory tour promoter Chuck Sullivan announced to members of the press the next cities on the tour's
agenda. Mile High Stadium in Denver, Colorado, had been
locked in for September 7 and 8, and the contracts had at
long last been signed for Washington, D.C., whose shows
were to be held on September 21 and 22. That night Sullivan
also told us that negotiations were still under way for the
weekend in between. "We've been approached by several
cities who are interested in hosting the Victory tour," smiled
Sullivan. Ultimately, the weekend in question turned out to
be the first Canadian date on the tour: Montreal, Quebec.

The agreement for Denver, Colorado, called for a third
night to be added to the weekend schedule in the form of
a Sunday concert. For this to happen, 90,000 tickets to the
Friday and Saturday shows had to be sold by Saturday,
September 1. By that date the minimum sales figure was
not met, so the event remained a two-night engagement.
However, according to the *Rocky Mountain News*, a local
daily newspaper, "First day sales on August 27 were re-

portedly in the 60,000 range, but dropped drastically after city officials announced a third concert also was possible. After Victory tour promoters said Saturday that sales fell short of the required 90,000 for a third performance, city officials said the figures were suspect and hinted they were contemplating legal action against the tour's organizers."

This was just another instance where the tour-planning timing was completely off. Had the contracts been signed sooner, there might have been time to sell out three Denver dates, but with the haphazard tour planning, virtually no preconcert promotion was possible, or attempted. During this same period of time, the fall tour by Prince was announced, and tickets were already on sale for November concerts. The Victory tour was paying for its last-minute bookings.

As it was, according to the contracts, the city of Denver stood to make quite a substantial profit from its two-day Jackson weekend. The gross estimate was for a profit of $460,000. Of that sum, $266,000 would be generated in seat tax, $100,000 would come from the rental of the stadium, $75,000 from the concession stands, and $20,000 in sales tax. Not bad.

HIS HOTNESS HOLDS A PRESS CONFERENCE

On Wednesday, September 5, Michael Jackson held a press conference in Hollywood to officially and publicly dispel all the rumors about his sex life, his plastic surgery, and the long-running tale that he has been taking female hormones to keep the pitch of his voice high. Although His Hotness was not present at the noontime event, both his personal manager, Frank Dileo, and his publicist, Norman Winter, were. The press conference came in the form of a carefully written two-page statement penned by Jackson, and read aloud by Dileo, to set the record straight "once and for all" about all the fables concerning Michael's personal life.

According to the statement, "It saddens me that many may actually believe the present flurry of false accusations. To this end, and I do mean END: No, I've never taken hormones to maintain my high voice! No, I've never had my cheekbones altered in any way! No, I've never had cosmetic surgery on my eyes! Yes, one day in the future I plan to get married and have a family. Any statements to the contrary are simply untrue."

Michael's statement continued, "As noted earlier, I love children. We all know that kids are very impressionable and therefore susceptible to such stories. I'm certain that some have already been hurt by this terrible slander. In addition to their admiration, I would like to keep their respect."

Within the same official statement, Michael said that the press conference was being held "based on the injustice of those allegations and the far-reaching trauma those who feel close to me are suffering."

Although Michael did not mention the all-too-obvious plastic surgery on his nose, he did conclusively draw up the guidelines as to which printed or stated facts about him he will and will not stand for. "As new fantasies are printed," stated Michael, his lawyers stand poised to "prosecute all guilty to the fullest extent of the law." I can already envision a front-page lawsuit brewing similar to the one that Carol Burnett waged and won against the *National Enquirer*.

According to Norman Winter, Michael was repeatedly advised not to hold the press conference, but "he was undaunted. He's been wanting to do this for a long time. He just decided he was going to once and for all come out and address these crazy charges." Added Winter, "If kids want to grow up and marry Michael Jackson, now they know they've got a chance."

DENVER, COLORADO

Friday, September 7, 1984, was a big night for concerts in Denver—better known as the Mile High City for its elevation above sea level. James Taylor was headlining Red Rocks Amphitheater, Elton John held court at McNichols Arena, while the Jacksons staged their Victory at Mile High Stadium.

Reported the next morning's *Denver Post*, Friday's sold-out crowd totaled 53,678 at Mile High Stadium while both Elton John and James Taylor also played their shows to capacity crowds of 14,000 and 9,000, respectively. It was a hot night for concerts in Denver in spite of the fact that the air was rather cool after sundown.

It had been formally announced that the one millionth Jacksons fan to see the Victory show would be in the audience the Monday night the Philadelphia show had been rained out. The tour promoters voided those 60,000 tickets on their tally and began counting up to one million from the beginning again. It was on Friday night in Denver that the one millionth Victory viewer was named. The lucky ticket holder was ten-year-old Sarah Petrakis, who was sitting in the audience with her mom and dad about one hundred yards from the stage.

Right before the show, Sarah and her parents were taken backstage to meet Michael Jackson and his brothers. To put the frosting on the cake, it was also Sarah's birthday! When she got backstage, Sarah had her picture taken with Michael, and even received a hug and a kiss from His Hotness. It is likely to be one birthday celebration Sarah Petrakis will never forget!

The same Friday night in Denver, a few minutes before 9:00 P.M., an announcement was made that due to unusually high winds, the aluminum frame of the TV video screen that usually was above the stage had become damaged and would not be used that evening for fear it might get blown down into the crowd and hurt someone. The news was roundly booed by the audience. However, at 9:04 when the house lights went down, the nonstop cheering and whistling from the crowd signaled the fact that TV screen was inconsequential compared to the prospect of seeing Michael Jackson in the flesh—at any distance.

The way that Mile High Stadium was set up for the Victory shows actually provided much better viewing than other stadiums——Philadelphia's JFK Stadium, for instance. The Denver setup featured two elevated sets of bleachers facing the stage in a V, plus a large amount of floor space.

Friday was a clear, almost cloudless night, and to the rear of the stage a bright and nearly full moon hung in the sky. The enthusiasm of the crowd was ferocious, and the Jacksons' famous entrance was still exciting for me to see, even at this, my twenty-fifth consecutive show!

On the last song of the night, "Shake Your Body (Down To The Ground)," Michael ad-libbed a couple of lines of "Don't Stop 'Til You Get Enough" into the song. All in all it was a great show and a great crowd. Once the show started, those who hadn't seen the show before with the video screen couldn't know anything was missing.

I attended all of the first thirty Victory shows accompanied by my pad and pen, and I usually looked quite conspicuous to people sitting around me as I wrote while Michael Jackson sang (don't worry——I can write without looking at the paper!). That Friday night I sat next to fourteen-year-old Melissa Wykoff and her two friends Tiffany and Yvette. Melissa told me that her mom had driven the trio of teenagers one hundred miles from Vale, Colorado, just to see the show. The three girls couldn't wait to give me their impressions afterward. "It was totally awesome!" Melissa gushed, "And Michael Jackson——I'm going to marry him!" Tiffany and Yvette, who were also fourteen, were already counting on being bridesmaids at the ceremony. I wondered if the bridesmaids would hold their bouquets with sequined gloves, and would the bride have on dark glasses instead of a veil. I guess we'll all have to wait and see!

Anyway, when I got upstairs to the press box, one of the first people I ran into was publicist Neil Friedman, who announced to me, "I've got something for your book!" and pointed to a row of three stitches across his forehead. It seems that in Philadelphia a TV cameraman from the local CBS affiliate wouldn't take no for an answer when he wanted to shoot video footage of the Jacksons at their hotel, and hit Neil with the camera! The real irony was that the brothers weren't even in the hotel when the cameraman insisted on access. Working in show business isn't always pretty!

That night at the regular post-show press briefing Chuck Sullivan fielded his usual questions from the local press about "the costliest show in the history of show business." Regarding the bumpy progress of the concert planning, Sullivan grinned and answered the query in typical football promoter's terms by admitting, "We've made some good plays, and we've made some bad plays!"

At 1:00 A.M. that same night, twenty-nine-year-old Darryl McGee fell through the ceiling over the gift shop at Denver's Fairmont Hotel downtown. He was desperately trying to find Michael Jackson's room when the mishap occurred. Accompanied to the hotel by his sixteen-year-old niece, Patrice, Darryl had already been thrown out of the hotel three times in an effort to meet the gloved one and introduce his niece. Pursued by angered security guards, McGee ran into an indoor fire escape, and spotted an air shaft. Forceably removing its cover, he climbed in and began walking across the suspended ceiling over the gift shop. The ceiling collapsed and McGee, who was unhurt, was arrested, and disappointed Patrice never did get to meet Michael Jackson. McGee, who admitted that he had had a few too many cocktails, was charged with criminal mischief but was released from custody on a $2,000 bond. A total of four hundred feet of the ceiling was damaged, and McGee promised not to give a repeat performance of his stunt.

On Saturday night in Denver, the video screen had been fixed and another sold-out crowd got their evening with the Thriller. It was fascinating to watch the same mixture of orderly Rocky Mountain-area audience members witness the same show, but this time I could watch how the video hookup was used to manipulate crowd response from the people who had seats up in the rafters.

Elton John, who performed only one night in Denver that weekend, was in Saturday night's Victory audience. In fact, there was a rumor that night that Elton and Michael might do a duet as an encore, but again it was only a rumor, and, alas, did not take place.

The fireworks at the end of the two shows in Denver were among the best on the tour. Also, due to the shorter days, the concerts were starting earlier and earlier in the evening. That Saturday's show was over by 10:40 P.M.

Naturally, there was a weekend-long vigil outside the Fairmont Hotel in downtown Denver. The Jackson entourage of stars had the entire twenty-fifth floor of suites to themselves, while other guests of the hotel included Elton John; and Debbie Reynolds, who gave a benefit concert to raise money for Rose Medical Center. On Sunday morning about thirty Jackson fans were still posted outside the hotel for a final look at the gloved one. At 11:30 A.M. when a white limousine pulled up in front of the Fairmont, Michael's fans were in ecstasy—until they found out it was there to pick up Debbie. "Who's Debbie Reynolds?" one young Jackson fanatic asked. After the throng of Jackson-maniacs went back to their posts, Reynolds slipped almost unnoticed into her awaiting limo.

Michael and the Jacksons left the Fairmont around 2:30 in the afternoon in two unmarked brown vans with dark windows and Colorado license plates. At that time Denver city officials were still investigating the ticket sales for that weekend to find out whether or not they were contractually owed a third concert from the Jacksons, as they were suspicious of the reported failure of 90,000 tickets to be sold by September 1.

According to Mark McCue, the chief desk clerk at the Fairmont Hotel, Michael and the Jackson brothers were so taken by the red-and-black-with-gold-braid-trim uniforms that the bellhops wear that they inquired about obtaining them. Unfortunately, the hotel didn't have any small enough to fit the interested brothers. When Michael stayed in New York City in July, he had successfully obtained one of the elaborate gold-braid-decorated hotel attendant's costumes from the Helmsley Palace for his private collection. Said

McCue of the Jacksons, "They love our bell uniforms. They think they're punk!"

So concluded Michael's otherwise victorious Rocky Mountain adventure. Next stop: Canada.

HOORAY FOR HOLLYWOOD!

After seeing Michael Jackson's astounding performances in his 1983 "Billie Jean," "Beat It," and "Thriller" videos, it was evident to me that full-length feature films represented the next horizon for him to embark upon. Michael's charisma is only enhanced and magnified by the camera. And with the astonishing box-office success of Prince's 1984 movie debut in *Purple Rain*, the interest in rock and roll movie musicals has suddenly reached new heights. It was only a matter of time before Michael starred in a film of his own. There of course had been talk of Michael playing the title role in a new film version of Peter Pan with Steven Spielberg in the director's chair, but it seemed as if it was taking forever to negotiate.

The second week in September, it was at long last announced that Michael had signed a movie contract with Columbia Pictures. The agreement called for two films from Michael. The first one was to be called *They've Landed*, and it would star Michael and co-star his brothers. The plot of *They've Landed* was to be based on the song and video presentation of "Beat It"—sort of a jazzy *West Side Story*-type epic. The second theatrical film would star Michael solo, property to be decided upon and announced at a later date. According to the senior vice president of Columbia Pictures, Robert Lawrence, the exact plots of each of the films as of that date were "both in the formative stages."

ON AND OFF IN PITTSBURGH

With the beginning of the fall football season, it was becoming increasingly difficult for Stadium Management Corporation to finalize bookings at huge outdoor football arenas. An engagement tentatively set for October 13 and 14 was clear—there was no scheduling conflict. But there were a new set of problems. First of all, the tunnel that would be used to get the Jacksons' semitrailers into the stadium was too small. When Michael Baldy, director of operations at Pittsburgh's Three Rivers Stadium, announced that it would cost $30,000 to $50,000 to raise the ceiling of the tunnel, the Stadium Manager, Rick Bjorklund, said that the Jacksons would have to pay for the reconstruction. Chuck Sullivan retorted that in other cities the stadiums footed the bill for any structural problems.

However, the real stumbling block in obtaining a signed contract was the unionized souvenir vendors who have a contract with Three Rivers Stadium. Stadium Management Corporation employed its own T-shirt and program sellers, but Three Rivers Stadium refused to let their regular vendors off for the weekend, and the union wouldn't let them be pushed aside without pay. Chuck Sullivan even tried to bribe the vendors with $1,000 apiece to get lost on the proposed Victory weekend, but he was outvoted by the vendors 46 to 5. Said outraged Three Rivers Stadium vendor Edward Kirkwood, "Who do they think they are anyway?" Needless to say, Pittsburgh had to be dropped from the Jacksons' tour schedule.

MONTREAL BECOMES VILLE DE JACKSON

Montreal, Quebec, became the first Canadian city to host the Victory tour. As one of the largest North American cities, Montreal is a cultured and cosmopolitan metropolis where the arrival of Michael and his brothers was feted as though they were visiting royalty. As French is the official language of Quebec, the signs outside of open-air Olympic Stadium all heralded the appearance of "Les Jackson," in the Gallic spelling.

It was truly a big week for celebrities in Montreal, as the Victory concerts were held the same week that Pope

John Paul II visited the city. In fact the Pope used the Jacksons' Victory stage base at a rally that was held at Olympic Stadium the Tuesday preceding their sold-out Sunday and Monday shows.

Sitting in the middle of Olympic Stadium on Sunday night, September 16, it was difficult for me to imagine that only two months previous I was roasting alive in Texas Stadium. That night the thermometer dipped down into the thirties, making it decidedly cold in Montreal. I clutched a paper cup full of hot coffee to keep my hands warm, and imagined how on earth this tour was going to continue to play outdoor dates through December 1984 as planned. In Montreal when fans purchased official Jacksons sweat shirts, it wasn't merely as a souvenir—it was partially to have another layer of clothing to wear for warmth!

When the lights went down at 9:20 P.M. that Sunday night, the video reception didn't work at all. It was like watching TV when the horizonal hold flutters uncontrollably. As the show proceeded, many attempts to fix it failed. Because of the Canadian currency exchange rate, the ticket cost that night was forty Canadian dollars, so there were many irate fans who couldn't see any of the details of the show. Massive and ultramodern Olympic Stadium is so big that additional banks of speakers had to be set up on the field so that spectators in the uppermost, farthest-back sections could hear the music.

To compound the problems with the cold and the faulty video screen, during Michael's show-stopping "She's Out Of My Life," it began to rain! As Michael disappeared from the stage and Jermaine launched into "Let's Get Serious," the rain really picked up. Freezing cold and wet, I stood on my chair trying to see over the heads in front of me and thought to myself, "Let's get serious—it can't *really* be raining!" But by the end of Jermaine's "Dynamite" the rain was over. And by the time Michael came back to the stage with "Tell Me I'm Not Dreamin' (Too Good To Be True)," the video hookup was miraculously fixed. When the close-ups of the stage activity finally hit the giant screen, the crowd went berserk with excitement!

When Michael and Marlon made their grand reappearance on "Beat It," you could actually see the condensation from Michael's breath magnified on the screen—it was that cold.

As an added treat, during "Shake Your Body (Down To The Ground)," Jackie Jackson came out on stage to sing with his brothers in the finale. Dressed in a white sequined jacket over a red top and black pants, Jackie hobbled out with a cane to clap and sing along with Michael, Marlon, Randy, Tito, and Jermaine. This marked the first time during the tour that all six Jackson brothers had been on stage and in costume for the finale. By the way Jackie grabbed Michael's hand midsong, it looked like his appearance was impromptu, and as much of a surprise to Michael as to the audience. Jackie's sudden on-stage arrival from the wings was totally unannounced, unheralded, and also unnoticed by the vast majority of the crowd. It was obvious from the way he limped off stage that he had not yet fully recovered from his knee surgery.

Following Sunday night's performance, Michael met the preteen children of new Canadian Prime Minister Brian Mulroney in his room at the Four Seasons (Quatre Saisons) hotel. The invitation had been extended by Michael's manager, Frank Dileo, to First Lady Mila Mulroney at the show.

The Monday night, September 17, Montreal show was again a sellout, drawing in excess of 55,000 cheering fans. In fact, about 100 people tried unsuccessfully to crash the gates. The show itself ran much more smoothly than the night before: the video setup worked from the very beginning, it didn't rain, and it was warmer. Again at the finale, Jackie made a guest appearance. "Jackie!" announced Michael this time as the elder Jackson brother arrived on stage for "Shake Your Body (Down To The Ground)." During the song, Jackie led the crowd in the "make a V for Victory" clap-along that Marlon usually presided over. Jackie even abandoned his cane to do a few light dance steps in unison with his siblings. He also tossed the tambourine that he had been playing to some lucky fan on the "terrain" level of the audience.

MORE MICHAEL DETAILS

In late September, it was announced which charities would be the recipients of Michael Jackson's earnings from the Victory tour. The three worthy recipients are the United Negro College Fund, Camp Good Times (a camp for children who are cancer patients), and the T. J. Martell Foundation for Leukemia and Cancer Research. Although the exact financial disclosure wasn't made, it is expected that approximately five million dollars will be divided between these three charities.

For the three months that I covered the first thirty Victory shows, no one else who wasn't an employee of the show in some way saw as many performances as I did. However, my main running mates in the journalist circle were Miles White (*USA Today*) and James McBride (*People*). On the local level, Gary Graff (the *Detroit Free Press*) and Kevin Bezner (the *Jacksonville Journal*) wrote the most Jackson-related stories for their publications. However, it was in Montreal that I must say I had to award the "Anything for a Story" prize to Thomas Schnurmacher for publishing a complete list of Michael Jackson's dirty laundry in the September 18, 1984, issue of the local daily newspaper the *Gazette*.

It seems that the Thriller's Montreal laundry included: 3 sweaters, 10 pair of pants, 4 sports shirts, 9 T-shirts, 13 pairs of white jockey shorts, and 15½ pairs of socks. Yes, it's true. Even Michael Jackson occasionally loses one sock! The laundry traveled from Michael's $790-per-night suite at the Four Seasons to the Bellingham Cleaners by stretch limousine. Now, that's what I call class!

CHAPTER THIRTEEN

WASHINGTON D.C. AND BEYOND

The September 21 and 22, 1984, Victory tour dates were the last of the consecutive shows I attended. At this point in the tour I knew every light cue, musical note, and detail of the show by heart. In fact, I could almost moonwalk! Since September 23 was the first official full day of autumn, it seemed like a logical cutoff point from which to report my findings to the world.

All 90,000 tickets for both of the Jacksons' performances at Washington, D.C.'s Robert F. Kennedy Stadium sold out in three short days. I had naturally figured that since Michael was playing the nation's capital, that Ron and Nancy (Reagan) would surely be in attendance. However, Chuck Sullivan's right-hand man, former Army Captain Bob Sullivan, announced to the press that the President and First Lady not only weren't invited to attend, but would have to wait in line for tickets just like everybody else! Now, that's what I call completely tacky behavior on the part of the promoters.

In the Tuesday, September 18, issue of the *Washington Post*, I counted 185 separate classified ads advertising

"TICKETS—JACKSONS" for sale, and ranging in price from $39 to $300 each, depending upon location. As in all the cities that the tour played, there were many scalpers roaming the grounds in front of RFK Stadium from early in the day of the shows on up to show time. Sometimes bargains could be found if one didn't mind waiting until the show had already begun, but more times than that there were many disappointed bargain-hunting fans who had to be satisfied listening to the music and cheering from outside the stadium gates.

Michael Jackson's fascination with Broadway, theater, and show business in general extended to his activities on the road. In his usual dark glasses and fedora disguise, Michael went book shopping while in Montreal and purchased the following titles: *Costume Cavalcade*, *The History of Costume*, *Scene Design*, and *Stravinsky in the Theater*. And when he arrived in Washington, Michael slipped into the Kennedy Center Opera House to catch Anthony Quinn and Lila Kedrova in the touring production of *Zorba*. Michael sat in the Presidential Box with Presidential counselor Ed Meese. Although Michael made his usual incognito, through-the-back-way entrance to his seat, the cast caught wind of Jackson's attendance. Said *Zorba* cast member Steven Yuhasz, "They tried to keep it from Mr. Quinn—it's a distraction," but, he added, "Everyone was joking around, saying, 'Okay, get out the white gloves for the opening number.'"

During his stay in Washington, Michael and family took up residence at the Regent Hotel in the Georgetown area of the city. The hotel is distinguished as Washington D.C.'s only top-rated "five star" hotel in terms of poshness and elegance. As in other stops along the way, Michael went book shopping—this time at a store called Yesterday Books, where his most significant purchase was a photo book on Judy Garland and Liza Minnelli. And before Saturday's show Michael met the three winners of an anti-drunk-driving essay-writing competition at a dinner held in their honor, also at the Regent Hotel.

On Friday, September 21, the twenty-ninth edition of the Victory show had something new added to it. Directly following Chris Bliss's juggling act and just before the lights went up for the pre-Jacksons intermission, the "Torture" video was played on the screen that crowns the massive stage. The video proved quite successful at even further inciting the crowd, and at this moment the show at last in some way acknowledged the album that the tour had been named after. At 9:21 P.M. Jackie, dressed in a pair of black multizippered parachute pants and a white sequined top, appeared on stage with his cane to wave to the crowd. Six minutes later the show began.

The Washington audience was very enthusiastic, and the 70-degree weather made for a smoothly running and perfectly executed show. Since the show debuted in Kansas City, a new hydraulic-lift platform had been added to the front of the stage, so that Michael could safely come even closer to his adoring fans amid his touching "She's Out Of My Life." At the show's 11:20 ending, an impressive array of fireworks lit up the sky overhead in a flashy fashion befitting the nation's capital. As the house lights went up and the show ended, a tape of "Torture" was played over the loudspeakers, plugging the song even more. Jackie didn't sing or dance at either of the D.C. shows as he had done earlier in the week in Montreal. In the audience that night were such luminaries as Mike Love of the Beach Boys, Peaches of the singing duo Peaches and Herb, Eva Gabor, and Ethel Kennedy.

Victory concert number thirty was held on September 22, and since it was the last consecutive show I would be seeing, I decided to venture over to the site of the show a bit early just to fully experience the scene in its entirety. When I arrived at RFK Stadium at 4:30 P.M., the sidewalks in the area already teemed with vendors selling hot dogs, posters, buttons, cheap binoculars, necklaces, incense, balloons, sequined and/or glitter-covered white gloves, and in fact just about every sort of unauthorized item on which one could possibly stamp, print, or post Michael Jackson's image and/or name. It looked like a circus had come to town—and in a way it had. However, not even P. T. Barnum could have hoped to rake in the kind of cash that the Victory tour was bringing in—authorized or not!

One inventive trio even had a full-color Michael Jackson cardboard cutout figure, and for $4 you could stand next to life-sized cardboard Michael and have an instant Polaroid photo taken with him. When I declined purchasing a snapshot with the two-dimensional Michael cutout, the cameraman yelled out, "Well, if you wander back, you know where Michael will be!"

That Saturday night the show again proceeded very smoothly, and there were no problems or deviations in its repertoire or astounding energy level. Jackie again came out front to wave, and then it was on with the show. Michael, as in the twenty-nine shows I had seen before, virtually dominated the on-stage energy with his high-voltage presence, his kinetic dancing, and his mesmerizing singing style. As far as I'm concerned, he is a showman par excellence.

MICHAEL JACKSON TRIVIA

While I was avidly following Michael Jackson and his family on the road, I was able to learn all sorts of little-known Victory tour facts. I'm certain that some future edition of "Trivial Pursuit" will be asking you some of these hot little items, so just for the record, here goes:

—On the inside of the black fedora hats that Michael tossed to the crowd every night during "Billie Jean" are the following words: "Made Expressly for Michael Jackson by Maddest Hatter/100% Genuine Fur."

—"Jacksonberg." That's the term that was given to the area where the Victory tour trucks were parked in each city.

—"The Tower of Babble." That's what the tour crew

referred to as the fifty-four-foot-high sound mixing and spotlight tower that stood in the middle of the field (everywhere but at Madison Square Garden).

—Huge black plastic sheets were used to cover the unsellable seats to the rear of the tower so that when Michael looked out into the audience from the stage, he wouldn't see any empty seats. Such a sight might upset the gloved one's performance!

—If you were cleaning up Michael Jackson's hotel room after he stayed there, what would you be likely to find littered about the room? The answer: popcorn! It's Michael's favorite snack and it's rarely available from room service, even from the poshest of hotels!

Also during the month of September, there were some new Jackson family developments. On September 7, Michael's eighteen-year-old younger sister Janet eloped and was married to twenty-one-year-old James DeBarge of the Motown singing group DeBarge. No other members of the Jackson family were present at the ceremony, which took place in secrecy in Grand Rapids, Michigan. On that same day, it was announced that Jermaine was suing his accounting firm for exorbitant fees deducted from his Victory tour earnings.

Although the sales of the hit single "State Of Shock" and the Jacksons' *Victory* album seemed slow at first, both were certified gold, and the album was also simultaneously certified platinum by the RIAA (Recording Industry Association of America). That early September announcement further validated the Jacksons' claim as the most successful musical group of 1984.

THE CONCERT OF THE CENTURY

After seeing three solid months and thirty Victory shows in a row, it was time for me to go back to my post as editor-in-chief of *Modern Screen* magazine where I write about the lives and loves of the movie stars. For Michael Jackson, his future included completing his family-reunion tour and becoming a bona fide movie star himself! The Victory tour went on to conquer more audiences across North America on into the fall of 1984, and I solidified my plans to finish off my Victory experience by attending the last concert in the last city of the tour.

Throughout these past two years of intense Michael Jackson-mania, I can honestly say that I have nothing but admiration for his talent, his creativity, and his indefatigable energy. On these pages I feel that I have faithfully paid tribute to the number-one superstar of the decade and the most successful personality in the history of show business. As a journalist, I have also presented many of the blunders, controversies, and decidedly negative aspects of the Victory tour. These tour-planning troubles have in no way altered my respect or admiration for Michael Jackson. My respect for him is not only intact, it has been enhanced. Anyone who would donate 100 percent of his profits from the Victory tour to charity truly has to have a heart as golden as his hit records.

I have loved every minute of my three months of following Victory into every single city where it landed during July, August, and September 1984. Even after thirty times of witnessing Michael's performance of "Billie Jean," it still knocks me out. This has truly been the most expensive, most profitable, the grandest, and most talked about concert tour ever planned, mounted, and executed. Once Michael Jackson hit stage, all the problems that plagued the tour planning vanished. And from the first "Wanna Be Startin' Something" of the show, there was no doubt who the hottest superstar in the world is.

He's the Thriller, he's the gloved one, he's His Hotness, he's the best-selling singing superstar the world has ever seen. He's Michael Jackson!

VICTORY TOUR CREDITS:

PEPSI-COLA Presents
A Don King/Joseph & Katherine Jackson Event
Promoted by Stadium Management Corporation
(headed by Chuck Sullivan)
Produced by Jacksons Entertainment Corporation
In Association With
Larry Larson
Written & Designed by MICHAEL JACKSON

Starring:
THE JACKSONS: JACKIE, JERMAINE, MARLON, MICHAEL, RANDY, & TITO

The musicians:

Keyboards	Rory Kaplan
Keyboards	Pat Leonard
Drums	Jonathan Moffett
Guitars	David Williams
Keyboards	Jai Winding
Guitars	Gregg Wright

The crew:

Staging Design Executor	Ian Knight
Production Manager	Peyton Wilson
Stage Manager	Mike Hirsh
Assistant Stage Manager	Pee Wee Jackson
Lighting Design	Robert A. Roth & James K. Chapman for Space Point Design
Stage Construction & Engineering	John McGraw & Planview, Inc.

Robotic Lighting Design . . . . Michael Jackson
Robotic Lighting Execution. . . . . . . Applied Entertainment
Systems
Lighting Company . . . . TASCO
Site Coordinators . . . . Bugzee Hougdahl & Jose Ward
Sound Company. . . . . Clair Brothers Audio
House Mixers. . . . . M. L. Procise & Mike Stahl
Laser Effects. . . . . Showlasers, Inc., Dallas, Texas
Specialty Costume Design . . Michael Jackson & Ted Shell
Jackson Costume Design . . . . Bill Whitten
Musician Costume Design. . . . . Enid Jackson
Magic Illusion Design . . . . Franz Harary
Pyro Effects . . . . M.P. Associates
Stage Scaffolding . . . . Mountain Productions
Scenic Scrims . . . . FM Productions
Video . . . . Pictures Inc.
Video Director . . . . Sandy Fullerton
Tour Trucking. . . . . Upstaging
Musical Support. . . . . Yamaha

Opening Overture:

Written by Michael Jackson, Jai Winding & Pat Leonard
Produced by . . . . Michael Jackson & Jai Winding
Arranged by . . . . Marty Paich & Jerry Hey
Michael Jackson's Management. . . . . Frank Dileo
The Jacksons' Management . . . . Jack Nance
Tour Consultant. . . . . Irv Azoff & MCA Inc.
Road Manager. . . . . Nelson Hayes

Legal Representation:

Michael Jackson. . . . . John Branca & Gary Stiffleman
Jermaine Jackson. . . . . Joel Katz
The Jacksons. . . . . Lee Phillips & Peter Paterno

Press Representation:

Michael Jackson. . . . . Norman Winter/Associates
The Jacksons. . . . . Howard Bloom Organization
Tour Photographer . . . . Harrison Funk
Security Director . . . . Bill Bray
Representative for Pepsi-Cola. . . . . Ken Ross

Backstage Ambiance Director .... Don Lyon
Michael's Personal Chef.................. Mani Khalsa
Victory Tour Chef .... Cy Kocis

DISCOGRAPHY

ALBUMS:

Michael Jackson with The Jackson Five:

—*Diana Ross Presents The Jackson Five* (Motown), 1969*
—*ABC* (Motown), 1970*
—*Third Album* (Motown), 1970
—*The Jackson Five Christmas Album* (Motown), 1970*
—*Maybe Tomorrow* (Motown), 1971
—*Goin' Back To Indiana* (TV soundtrack—Motown), 1971*
—*The Jackson Five's Greatest Hits* (Motown), 1971*
—*Lookin' Through The Windows* (Motown), 1972*
—*Skywriter* (Motown), 1973
—*Get It Together* (Motown), 1973
—*Dancing Machine* (Motown), 1974*
—*Moving Violation* (Motown), 1975
—*Joyful Jukebox Music* (Motown), 1975
—*The Jackson Five Anthology* (3-record set—Motown), 1976*
—*Boogie* (Natural Resources/Motown), 1979
—*Motown Superstar Series, Volume 12: The Jackson Five* (Motown), 1980
—*Michael Jackson & The Jackson Five: Great Songs And Performances That Inspired The Motown 25th Anniversary T.V. Special* (Motown), 1983
—*Michael Jackson And The Jackson Five: 14 Greatest Hits* (reissued songs on a "picture disk" with a white glitter

*Gold album (for 500,000 units sold in the U.S.).

glove, and color poster included—(Motown), 1984
—*The Great Love Songs Of The Jackson Five* (Motown), 1984

Michael Jackson with The Jacksons:

—*The Jacksons* (Epic/Philadelphia International), 1976*
—*Goin' Places* (Epic/Philadelphia International), 1977
—*Destiny* (Epic), 1978**
—*Triumph* (Epic), 1978
—*The Jacksons Live* (2-record set—Epic), 1981
—*Victory* (Epic), 1984**
—*Victory* (the picture disk) (Epic), 1984

Michael Jackson with The Jackson Five on compilations and other albums, performing material not found anywhere else:

—*Motown At The Hollywood Palace* (live performances of "I Want You Back" and medley "Sing A Simple Song/Can You Remember"—Motown), 1970
—*Diana: TV Soundtrack* (the Jackson Five sing two live medleys: "Mama's Pearl"/"Walk On By"/"The Love You Save," "I'll Be There"/"Feelin' Alright"; Michael and his brothers are also featured in a skit with Diana Ross and Bill Cosby—Motown), 1971
—*The Motown Story* (Michael talks about his life in the Jackson Five—Motown), 1970
—*Motown Superstars Sing Motown Superstars* (previously unreleased "Ask The Lonely" by the Jackson Five—Motown), 1983

*Gold album (for 500,000 units sold in the U.S.).
**Platinum album (for 1,000,000 units sold in the U.S.).

Michael Jackson:

—*Got To Be There* (Motown), 1972
—*Ben* (Motown), 1972*
—*Music & Me* (Motown), 1973
—*Forever, Michael* (Motown), 1975
—*The Best Of Michael Jackson* (Motown), 1975
—*Off The Wall* (Epic), 1979**
—*Motown Superstar Series, Volume 7: Michael Jackson* (Motown), 1980
—*One Day In Your Life* (Motown), 1981
—*E.T. The Extra-Terrestrial Storybook* (MCA), 1982†
—*Thriller* (Epic), 1982**†
—*Thriller* (the picture disk—Epic), 1983
—*Thriller* (half-speed master version—Epic), 1983
—*Farewell My Summer Love* (previously unreleased material originally recorded in 1973—Motown), 1984
—*The Great Love Songs Of Michael Jackson* (Motown), 1984

Michael on Movie Soundtracks:

—*The Wiz* (2-record set—MCA), 1978

*Gold album (for 500,000 units sold in the U.S.).
**Platinum album (for 1,000,000 units sold in the U.S.).
†Grammy Award-winner.

SINGLES:

Michael Jackson with The Jackson Five:

—*I Want You Back* (Motown), 1969**
—*ABC* (Motown), 1970**
—*The Love You Save/Found That Girl* (Motown), 1970**
—*I'll Be There* (Motown), 1970**
—*Mama's Pearl* (Motown), 1971*
—*Never Can Say Goodbye* (Motown), 1971*
—*Maybe Tomorrow* (Motown), 1971
—*Sugar Daddy* (Motown), 1971*
—*Little Bitty Pretty One* (Motown), 1972
—*Lookin' Through The Windows* (Motown), 1972
—*Corner Of The Sky* (Motown), 1972*
—*Hallelujah Day* (Motown), 1973
—*Get It Together* (Motown), 1973
—*Dancing Machine* (Motown), 1974**
—*Whatever You Got, I Want* (Motown), 1974
—*I Am Love, parts 1 and 2* (Motown), 1975
—*Forever Came Today* (Motown), 1975

Michael Jackson with The Jacksons:

—*Enjoy Yourself* (Epic), 1976*
—*Show You The Way To Go* (Epic/Philadelphia International), 1977
—*Goin' Places* (Epic/Philadelphia International), 1977
—*Blame It On The Boogie* (Epic), 1978
—*Shake Your Body (Down To The Ground)* (Epic), 1979**
—*Lovely One* (Epic), 1980

*Gold single (for 1,000,000 units sold in the U.S.).
**Platinum single (for 2,000,000 units sold in the U.S.).

—*Heartbreak Hotel* (Epic), 1980
—*Can You Feel It* (Epic), 1981
—*Walk Right Now* (Epic), 1981
—*Torture* (Epic), 1984

Michael Jackson and Diana Ross:

—*Ease On Down The Road* (MCA), 1978

Michael Jackson and Paul McCartney:

—*The Girl Is Mine* (Epic), 1982*
—*Say, Say, Say* (Epic), 1983

Michael Jackson, The Jacksons, and Mick Jagger:

—*State Of Shock* (Epic), 1984*

Michael Jackson:

—*Got To Be There* (Motown), 1971*
—*Rockin' Robin* (Motown), 1971*
—*I Wanna Be Where Your Are* (Motown), 1972
—*Ben* (Motown), 1972**
—*With A Child's Heart* (Motown), 1973
—*We're Almost There* (Motown), 1975
—*Just A Little Bit Of You* (Motown), 1975
—*You Can't Win, part 1* (Epic), 1979

*Gold single (for 1,000,000 units sold in the U.S.).
**Platinum single (for 2,000,000 units sold in the U.S.).

—*Don't Stop 'Til You Get Enough* (Epic), 1979*†
—*Rock With You* (Epic), 1979*
—*Off The Wall* (Epic), 1979*
—*She's Out Of My Life* (Epic), 1980*
—*One Day In Your Life* (Motown), 1980
—*Billie Jean* (Epic), 1983*†
—*Beat It* (Epic), 1983*†
—*Wanna Be Startin' Something* (Epic), 1983*
—*Human Nature* (Epic), 1983
—*P.Y.T. (Pretty Young Thing)* (Epic), 1983
—*Thriller* (Epic), 1984*
—*Farewell My Summer Love* (Motown), 1984

Michael Jackson 12" Disco Remixes:

—*Billie Jean* (Epic), 1983
—*Wanna Be Startin' Something* (Epic), 1983
—*Say, Say, Say* (with Paul McCartney—Epic), 1983
—*Thriller* (Epic), 1984
—*State Of Shock* (with The Jacksons and Mick Jagger —Epic), 1984
—*Torture* (The Jacksons) (Epic), 1984

Michael Jackson Guest Appearances

  As Producer:
  —"Night Time Lover" on the LaToya Jackson debut album, *LaToya Jackson* (Polydor), 1980
  —"Muscles" on the Diana Ross album *Silk Electric* (RCA), 1982
  —"Centipede" on the Rebbie Jackson album *Centipede* (Epic), 1984

*Gold single (for 1,000,000 units sold in the U.S.).
**Platinum single (for 2,000,000 units sold in the U.S.).
†Grammy Award-winner.

As a Guest Duet Artist:

—On the Paul McCartney album *Pipes Of Peace* ("Say, Say, Say" with Paul McCartney; "The Man" with Paul McCartney—Columbia), 1983

—On the Rockwell album *Somebody's Watching Me* ("Somebody's Watching Me" with Rockwell—(Motown), 1984

—On the Jermaine Jackson album *Jermaine Jackson* ("Tell Me I'm Not Dreamin' [Too Good To Be True]" with Jermaine Jackson—Arista), 1984

Compact Disks:

—*Triumph* (The Jacksons) (Epic), 1983

—*Off The Wall* (Michael Jackson) (Epic), 1983

—*Thriller* (Michael Jackson) (Epic), 1983

—*Michael Jackson and The Jackson Five: Compact Command Performance* (Motown), 1984

—*Victory* (The Jacksons) (Epic), 1984

Music Videos:

—"Can You Feel It" (with The Jacksons), 1981

—"Billie Jean," 1983

—"Beat It," 1983

—"Say, Say, Say" (with Paul and Linda McCartney), 1983

—"Thriller," 1983

Video Disks and Video Cassettes:

—*The Wiz* (MCA/Universal), 1978

—"The Making of 'Michael Jackson's "Thriller"'" (Vestron Video), 1983

ABOUT THE AUTHOR

Mark Bego is currently Editor-In-Chief of the oldest and most famous show business fan magazine in existence, *Modern Screen*. A native of Detroit, Michigan, his interest in all aspects of show business has led *Cash Box* magazine to recently proclaim that "Bego is one of New York's finest entertainment writers!"

Mark's first Michael Jackson biography, *Michael!* (Pinnacle Books, 1984) sold three millions copies worldwide, also appearing in five non-American editions: British (Zomba Books), French (Editions Carrere), French mass market (Hachette), Japanese (Shinshokan), and Hebrew (Triwaks Enterprises). The book was also serialized in America (the *Star* and the *Los Angeles Times* Syndicate), Britain (*No. 1*), Spain (*Cosmopolitan*), Portugal (*Bloch Editores*), and France (*France Soir*). In 1984 his radio and television interviews on Jackson-mania and the entertainment world were broadcast to every continent in the world, including being translated into Russian via Voice of America. The American edition of *Michael!* spent six weeks on the *New York Times* best-seller list.

In addition to *Michael!* and *On The Road With Michael!* Mark is also the author of three other published books, *Barry Manilow* (Grosset & Dunlap/Tempo Books, 1977), *The Captain & Tennille* (Grosset & Dunlap/Tempo Books, 1977), and *The Doobie Brothers* (Popular Library, 1980).

Bego has critiqued records and concerts, reviewed Broadway shows, covered the Manhattan nightlife circuit, and interviewed media stars (including Rod Stewart, Cher, Katharine Hepburn, and Donna Summer) for such publications as *People*, *US*, *After Dark*, *Billboard*, *Record World*, and *Cue/New York*, to name a few.

Mark appeared weekly for two years as an on-camera reviewer and interviewer on the Manhattan television show *Tomorrow's Television Tonight*, and as a host and producer of his own TV special, *Profile*. He was the producer/performer/host of the recent New York City stage shows *Casino Evil* and *Stupid Cupid*. His articles in *Modern Screen* are read around the world.